Introduction to the
Constitutional History of Modern Greece

PREPARED UNDER
THE AUSPICES OF THE COLUMBIA
UNIVERSITY COUNCIL FOR RESEARCH
IN THE SOCIAL SCIENCES

Introduction to the Constitutional History of Modern Greece

NICHOLAS KALTCHAS

NEW YORK
COLUMBIA UNIVERSITY PRESS
1940

COPYRIGHT 1940
COLUMBIA UNIVERSITY PRESS, NEW YORK
Foreign Agents: OXFORD UNIVERSITY PRESS, *Humphrey Milford, Amen House, London, E.C. 4, England,* AND *B. I. Building, Nicol Road, Bombay, India;* MARUZEN COMPANY, LTD., *6 Nihonbashi, Tori-Nichome, Tokyo, Japan*

Manufactured in the United States of America

Preface

THESE PAGES on the constitutional history of modern Greece—pages that are brilliant both in matter and in manner—will interest several classes of readers. Here those who know and love Greece will find an authoritative account of her constitutional development, which, given the author's thesis—"the influence of foreign policy on domestic politics"—must needs be (and was) written by "a good European." Students of public law and institutions, for whom few political phenomena are without pertinence, will now have a volume which will not feel abashed if it finds that on the shelves its neighbors are works on constitutionalism in classical Greece. Then there are those readers who—subject apart—are always fascinated by the play of a fine mind on materials which it has mastered and which it can illumine.

There is, finally, a large group of readers who share one or more of the interests I have mentioned, but who will handle this volume reverently because they knew and loved Nicholas Kaltchas: fellow countrymen here and abroad, teachers, colleagues, students. It is to them, as one of them, that I address this Preface which they have privileged me to write. I devote it not to the following pages on constitutional history—a lily needs no gilding—but to its author, who, as brilliant a student as I have ever had, became my warm friend.

Nicholas Kaltchas entered Columbia University in the autumn of 1920—a year before I joined the Faculty of Political Science. While his chief interests were in the Department of History, he also took courses in sociology and economics and must have worked hard, because he wrote an excellent essay on "The General Election of 1906 in England," and the degree of Master of Arts was awarded him in June, 1921. During the following academic year, completing his residence for the degree of Doctor of Philosophy, he took several courses in the Department of Public Law, and it was then that I came to know him. His presence was such that an instructor's eye could not pass him by: short, stocky, almost swarthy; a shock of black hair; an expressive face, with a closely clipped moustache and flashing eyes, and sensitive hands. Silent, he was a striking figure. Participating in class discussion, he at once demonstrated a superior intelligence, broad knowledge, and an uncommon ability to marshal it and make it become wisdom. One who has taught for a quarter of a century has met many classes. Some are soon forgotten. Others remain vivid because they contained groups of outstanding students, or, more rarely, because of a single student of exceptional brilliance and sympathy, who could, without seeming to play a stellar role, serve as a yeast cake which made the binding dough of mediocrity arise to unexpected heights. I am not yielding to the temptation of lapidary exaggeration when I say that Kaltchas's class has never ceased to be vivid to me, not alone because of him but also because of others who were his friends and became mine.

As a graduate student he had, of course, great advantages. Classical Greece and her literature were his natural heritage, in him flowering in intellectual cultivation and tolerance of mind and heart. The world had already been harsh to him. Later it was to be even harsher, because he was rarely out of a shadow cast by ill health and made darker because his purse was never full. His day ended too soon and suddenly, but it was a day which was bright for his friends and was not bereft of satisfactions for himself.

Since in 1921 the world had already been harsh, it was no wonder that, even though no older than his fellow graduate students, he seemed more mature. Born in Strandja, East Thrace, Turkey, on March 30, 1895, Nicholas Kaltchas attended the Greek schools of Constantinople and in 1914 received his

Bachelor of Arts degree from Robert College, with a record as brilliant as any previous student had ever made. Inducted into the Turkish army in 1915, he served for three years and reached the rank of lieutenant. His military service did not advantage his health, which had never been robust, and he served without the solace, which so many millions of youths of his age had, of fighting for his own country. The war over, he engaged in newspaper work in Constantinople: on *Chronos,* a Greek daily; as a political writer for the *Orient News* (an English daily); and later as editor of the *Spectator.* In 1919 he came to the United States with an unofficial diplomatic mission of Thracian Greeks, and the next year, as I have said, he registered as a student at Columbia University.

When warm personal friendship began to dominate our relationship I cannot say; but in October, 1922, he was writing to me from Saranac, where he would have to return again and again: "I need not tell you that it is a great nuisance, this enforced idleness, and an even greater nuisance to find how easily one gets accustomed to it and allows it to degenerate into indolence. I am fighting this tendency as strenuously as my health will permit me and I hope that the end of my stay here next spring will not find me a confirmed idler." He was anxious about the safety of his family, who lived on the Asiatic side of Constantinople: "I am afraid my father's business in Thrace will be ruined as a result of the fighting that is sure to take place there just as it was ruined during the first Balkan war."

I venture to quote further at some length to show the flavor of his mind and the warmth of his heart: "The revolution in Greece has been beneficent only insofar as it has established, or will establish, a stronger government. It is naïve to believe that the abdication of Constantine will placate France. She is committed to the hilt to support the Turkish claims in Europe, and it is hard for her now to wiggle out of her engagements to Kemal even if she wants to. She will have a good excuse for doing so if Kemal insists on Russia's participation in the Conference, but then it will be too late. The Turks will already be in military occupation of Thrace, where they will serve as the vanguard of Soviet Imperialism, a revival of Czarist Imperialism in a deadlier form. Lloyd George and Churchill have brains and imagination enough to see the implications and consequences of the present trend of events, but they are hampered by a factious and unscrupulous press and by an electorate, especially the Labor part of it and also the Wee-Fees of the Asquith and Grey and Philip Gibbs type, that is very short-sighted and uneducated and stupid in foreign affairs. If Europe really desires peace—think of Poincaré as a pacifist!—the best way to secure it would be to keep the Turks in Asia with the Sea of Marmora and the Bosphorus and the Dardanelles between them and Europe. Once they are allowed to cross into Europe, there will be no peace in the Balkans. But no, that is not the way of the Allies! They will purchase peace at the price of the Turks, especially since it so happens that the price will be paid by Greece. Why did they not follow the same procedure in 1914 and avoid the Great War by giving Serbia to Austria and allowing Germany to annex Belgium? But then the Germans were 'barbarians' whereas the Turks ought to be given a chance to try their administrative abilities and exert their civilizing influence in Thrace just as they have done in Asia Minor! And speaking of Asia Minor, think what a howl would have gone up if Smyrna, instead of being a Greek and Armenian city, was inhabited by a more civilized race! French propaganda is still rife over Louvain and Rheims and the devastated regions. But the Smyrna horror, which was perpetrated only yesterday, has already been forgotten. Indeed, the French Foreign Office has actually accused the Greeks of Smyrna, on Turkish official evidence, of having burnt their own houses and left the Turkish quarter of the city intact! And to think that only five years ago, in France's darkest hour, the Greek people made a revolution, from the consequences of which they are still suffering, in order to help save France from her enemies, of whom the Turks, whom she has now befriended, were not the least tenacious. And now they talk of blockading Greece in order to coerce her into evacuating Thrace. Why a blockade? Let them send Foch to do it!"

There followed a word of apology for fear he had bothered me at too great length. "But I have to talk to somebody or I will 'bust up.' And then it may interest you to know how a Greek, who is not a very narrow nationalist, feels about it all."

By the following year he was well enough to serve as director of the Press Bureau of the Greek Legation in Washington. While at Saranac he had regretted that he had not taken his oral examinations on the subjects at the conclusion of his residence at Columbia University in 1922. He had then thought, too modestly I assured him, that he was not sufficiently prepared. In the spring of 1924 he took his examinations and passed them brilliantly.

Doctoral examinations were then somewhat more formal than they are now, but less formal than they had been when the Faculty's "founding fathers" were present in the flesh rather than simply dominant in spirit. Irrespective of the formality, for the average student the examinations were and are an ordeal: two hours of questioning, not on courses taken, but on fields of major and minor interest, by four to eight professors, with perhaps even farther-ranging questions posed by representatives of the departments under the Faculty in which the candidate had not been a student. They attend to restrain the possible tolerance of the chiefly interested departments.

Some of these "orals," unhappily, are gall for the student and wormwood for the examiners. The two hours Kaltchas spent with his examiners were a causerie rather than an examination. There was talk between equals rather than between a student and teachers. Only once or twice in my experience of these examinations has a committee ever paid the candidate the compliment of having no discussion of his performance and of making an immediate announcement of the result of the examination.

That, I recall vividly, was the case with Kaltchas. That he could write a brilliant dissertation was plain. When he would be strong enough to do it was uncertain.

Anxious for a university career rather than for one in journalism or with his government, he accepted an instructorship in modern European history in the University of Montana. He was not too happy about this "from the strictly academic point of view," but the climate "is just what I need to recover my health completely." His health did improve, but knowing his intellectual capacity, he was eager to climb the academic ladder, and so when an opportunity came he moved to the University of Michigan, which he thought "loomed big and forbidding after Montana."

Whether he overworked or whether the Michigan climate did not permit as much activity as Montana's had, I do not know, but the result was another breakdown, and in May, 1926, again Saranac. At Michigan the historians had been much pleased with his teaching, and they held his post open for him. Writing to me on February 4, 1927, he said, "I am much better now, though far from completely well, and I intend to stay here until September, by which time I hope to have recovered sufficiently to go back to Michigan." But he feared the Michigan climate and knew that teaching again, so soon after his illness, would not be good for his lungs. In March he was reading the third and fourth volumes of Winston Churchill's *The World Crisis* and noting that they "lacked the literary finish" of the earlier volumes, but "were intensely vibrant and absorbing reading." Using the short intervals which were his daily allowance for "work" he completed a review which had "literary finish" and was "vibrant," but which avoided both presumption and pettiness in its judgments.

Then the clouds showed a silver lining. Columbia University's few fellowships under the Faculty of Political Science are usually reserved for "graduate students." But Kaltchas was an unusual person, and even though he had been away from the University for five years, we awarded him a Gilder Fellowship so that he might complete his dissertation. If health permitted, he was to go to Greece; it did not, so Kaltchas remained in this country and worked as much as he could on a monograph which had the tentative title "The Republican Constitution of Greece." Meanwhile his pen was not idle in other directions. He prepared for the *Foreign Policy Bulletin* an interesting research report on Roumania, "Another Little Entente Crisis?" and published in Greek a short introduction to the History of the United States (1928). Meanwhile he was not winning the battle against bad health. In November, 1929, he was at the New York State Sanatorium (less expensive than Saranac) and was helping the research members of the sanatorium staff by translating and abstracting medical papers from French and German. With the support of his Columbia friends, he applied for a Guggenheim fellowship. He hoped to go to Greece in order to complete his monograph. His application was unsuccessful, not because there was any doubt about his ability, but because the committee on awards naturally had misgivings about the possible state of his health. They accompanied the rejection of his application by word that if his health improved a future application might stand a much better chance. "I think," he said, "the committee's reluctance entirely justified (March, 1930)." But assistance came promptly from another quarter. In May the Columbia Council for Research in the Social Sciences made him a grant which, we hoped, would permit him to complete his monograph, and he sailed from New York in September.

In Athens, even though during November the weather was "unseasonably warm with the sun shining all day and the famous Attic sky perfectly cloudless," there were handicaps. "I have not felt very buoyant lately; and, I am afraid, if I permit my present mood to dictate this letter, I shall ruin irretrievably my reputation for 'cheerfulness' and 'courage.' " He had "one nasty cold after another. They are mere pin-pricks, of course; but, combined with my permanent ailment, they impair my efficiency and sap my morale."

In May, 1931, he was cabling that he was "feeling fit. Anxious work autumn," but his friends at Columbia could not turn up an academic post. That summer we missed seeing each other in Europe, but in September he was writing again from Saranac and assuming "that unless you have decided to attend the Geneva 'merry-go-round' to the bitter end, I assume you are now back home." Work on his monograph was proceeding. The first two chapters were drafted. He had assurances from the Michigan authorities that he could return there if he felt that he could stand a full-time schedule, but he was "perhaps unreasonably afraid of Ann Arbor, having broken down there twice." During the autumn he was in New York occasionally, and we saw a good deal of each other. The next year recognition came from his native country. M. Alexander Zaimis, the last president of the Republic of Greece, awarded him the silver cross of the Savior—"for scholarly work." Kaltchas wrote an article on the "Caliphate in Moslem Unity" for the Sunday New York *Times,* and he continued to make his expenses by tutoring and lecturing on European politics.

Heavy shadows fell over the Weimar Republic. The Bruning cabinet was struggling to preserve it and was governing by emergency ordinances under the famous Article 48 of the Republican Constitution. Kaltchas translated and analyzed the more important ordinances, and we published an article over our joint signatures in the *Political Science Quarterly*. There was some discussion of whether he would join the Columbia College staff in history—the only obstacles were New York City's climate and his health. Then a post in history and politics at Sarah Lawrence College became vacant. Kaltchas was appointed, and his friends were confident that this academic marriage would prove to be a happy one. We were not wrong.

Strength had to be husbanded. Summers had to be spent quietly in Saranac and Goshen. Work on the monograph had to be subordinated to teaching. In the autumn of 1935 Kaltchas took an apartment near the Grand Central Station in New York (commuting to Bronxville), and his New York friends were able to see him more frequently. He was anxious to go to Europe again, and there were proposals that he might write some articles on the Balkan conferences which the Carnegie Endowment for International Peace had sponsored. We thought that an examination of their organization and of their results by a scholar who was thoroughly familiar with the permutations and combinations of Balkan politics would be well worth while. But the proposals fell through.

The following summer (1937), however, he was able to go to Europe. From Switzerland ("it is dreadfully lonely here") he wrote in August that "somehow the world does not seem so agitated and so near the brink of disaster from Gstaad—or even from Paris—as it does from New York. I wonder if the much more efficiently sensational way we have in America of presenting the news has something to do with this." He spoke of Blum's overthrow by the French Senate (mentioned in his Introduction) and underlined his belief that more and more domestic politics and international relations were becoming inextricably connected, as Arnold Toynbee's last volumes of his *Survey* have argued in great detail. Returning to the United States two months later, he reported that his thesis "was nearly finished" and that he "would need about two week-ends to write a brief epilogue and as many more to verify my references." Just three weeks later he died, on Monday morning, October 25. The previous Friday he had as usual met his enthusiastic group of students.

Sometimes, I think, he must have lamented the fact that his talents were not being used by a great university for the training of graduate students. But no word of complaint ever came when he saw men mentally weaker, but physically stronger, rise to posts higher than the one he held and on whose tasks he spent himself to the limit. During those last years his students at Sarah Lawrence knew him best and admired him in full measure. He admired them, also, and frequently told me how keen and intelligent the best of them were. One of the latter must have written the tribute which appeared in the college paper *The Campus*:

"Nicholas Kaltchas will no longer teach at Sarah Lawrence. All that we can do is try to reconstruct a precise, clear picture of the man, and, taking the values which he believed and lived, try to incorporate them more fully into our own thinking. This, not mourning, is what he would wish.

"Nicholas Kaltchas often appeared to be a man who stood above the battle. In a deprecating way some of us used to call him 'that liberal.' Some would despair, 'How can man know so much and still refuse to take a stand with us!' But Kaltchas had a stand that he took and a line that he perpetually held. It cannot be described simply by the word 'liberal'; no one worked more earnestly nor adroitly than he to go beyond political labels to social realities. We must try to follow his example and discover the nature of his hard, lonely battle. For Kaltchas' students, Rousseau, for instance, became more than a writer of French fairy tales; he taught us to analyze Rousseau's writing until we saw that the beautiful concepts of the General Will and Social Contract could easily lead to Fascism. Though he hated Fascism as much as any of us, Kaltchas hated it for different reasons. He was not content to condemn it merely on the grounds of the vulgarized practical application, or the hysterical 'Mein Kampf' philosophy; he insisted that we go back to its roots. We had to read factual accounts of the breakdown of Social Democracy and the lofty philosophical origins in Spengler and Moeller von der Bruck before we were justified in condemning. In the same way he did not want us to feel justified in judging Communism before we had read Marx and Engels and Lenin and Trotzky.

"His whole theory of knowledge tied in with his rare art of teaching. His students were never bored or frightened by his erudition, since he had so well mastered his own field that he could popularize it and reduce it to our own terms. But we never found that he used this art unscrupulously by using deceptive oversimplification. When Kaltchas commented on a book or an idea he would always give a frank discussion of his own viewpoint on the subject and a concise report of it at face value. We felt that he had such a genuine respect for us as students, that he was content merely to give us diverse presentations of a truth and let us work out our own convictions.

"To know before one judged was the lesson that Kaltchas taught us. Last year the war and unreasoning hate of the world pushed into the campus. Some of us wondered if Kaltchas was not indulging in an inexcusable luxury, with his insistence on a reasonable analysis when the world was falling apart. We were irritated because talking to Kaltchas often made us realize what an emotional base many of our convictions had. Privately our irritation was tempered by a deep admiration for the man and the things he stood for. Unfortunately it was always easier, since we live at the peripheral level of political argument rather than personal relations, for us to convey our resentment. Now we cannot help hoping that in spite of his acceptance of our apparent resentment toward his viewpoint, Kaltchas was able to understand how much he meant to us. Through Kaltchas we learned that the values that he lived for were never more needed than they are today, when nations and well-meaning men are doing their best to destroy it.

"Kaltchas was a Greek in the alien land of America. But his isolation was more than that of a modern Greek patriot. He brought us the old Greek virtues of moderation and a belief in a certain inviolable truth. In the 'Apology' Plato has Socrates compare himself to the gad-fly that stirs the dull horse of the State into action. Today, when too many gad-flies are stirring the States and their inhabitants into unpremeditated compulsive action, another type of philosopher is needed along with the disciples of Socrates. Kaltchas was such a man, with the virtues of skepticism and restraint. He had a long, deep knowledge of cities and men.

"The death of Nicholas Kaltchas takes on a terrible symbolic meaning when we consider how few people are left in the world with the courage to live an intelligent, far-seeing, unimpassioned life."

As his teacher and friend, I can here find no exaggeration.

Those of us who still teach should hope that when our day is over, some student of ours, sincerely, understandingly, and eloquently, can give us as glowing an epitaph.

To Nicholas Kaltchas the world was the opposite of lenient. He lived most of his short adult life on the battlefield and in the hospital—not in universities or newspaper offices or chancelleries. When, too frequently, hard circumstances oppressed him and his friends grieved, he was not depressed; when, too rarely, the wave of fate carried him upward and his friends rejoiced, he was not exultant. Ofttimes triteness is so true that it cannot be improved upon, and so I simply say that Nicholas Kaltchas was a gentleman and a scholar.

LINDSAY ROGERS

Columbia University
August 8, 1940

Contents

	PREFACE, BY LINDSAY ROGERS	v
	INTRODUCTION	3
I.	SOURCES OF CONSTITUTIONALISM IN MODERN GREECE	9
II.	THE CONSTITUTIONS OF THE REVOLUTION	34
III.	THE CAPODISTRIAN DICTATORSHIP	58
IV.	THE FORFEITURE OF SOVEREIGNTY	80
V.	THE LIMITED MONARCHY OF OTHO	96
VI.	THE LIMITED DEMOCRACY OF GEORGE I	111
VII.	THE WORLD WAR AND THE CONSTITUTIONAL CRISIS IN GREECE	137
VIII.	POST-WAR DEVELOPMENTS	148
	BIBLIOGRAPHY	173
	INDEX	177

Introduction to the
Constitutional History of Modern Greece

Introduction

IN ONE of his suggestive essays, Professor A. F. Pollard contrasts the victory of constitutional and parliamentary government in England with the contemporaneous triumph of monarchical absolutism in France and attributes this difference to the comparative security which England derived from her geographical situation. Implicit in this thesis is the recognition of the close relationship between the international position of a given country and the development of its political institutions. This relationship was brought home to the average citizen during the World War of 1914–18, when the all-absorbing preoccupation with national security engendered even in the most liberal states an unprecedented expansion of governmental authority and the virtual suspension of constitutional government. It has been strikingly illustrated by such phenomena of post-war Europe as the rise of fascism and national socialism in the dissatisfied and the defeated countries, and more recently by the admittedly important part which the critical international situation played in inducing Premier Blum and the more responsible of his followers to accept defeat at the hands of the French Senate in the summer of 1937. But perhaps nowhere has the influence of foreign policy on domestic politics been more consistently and hence more impressively demonstrated than in the history of modern Greece.

This history, so far as it is the product of non-material forces, has been shaped by two parallel ideologies—nationalism and constitutionalism. The former has been motivated by a consciousness of distinctness and superiority reared upon the glory of classical Greece and the grandeur of the Byzantine Empire and reinforced by the acknowledged primacy of the Greeks among the Christians subject to Ottoman rule. Hence, when translated into a national policy, it has aimed to effect the political restoration of Hellenism to a status worthy of its past and in keeping with its contemporaneous cultural importance. Greek constitutionalism, on the other hand, has been grounded in the traditional association of the classical city state with liberty and democracy and, more substantially, in the long practice of communal self-government under the Ottoman Empire. It emerged, simultaneously with the national insurrection of 1821, in the theoretical verbiage made familiar on the Continent by the French Revolution, and it found a propitious soil in the speculative bent of the Greek mind and in the increasingly middle-class composition of Greek society. But while a consistently potent and at times an explosive factor, constitutionalism in Greece has been essentially subordinate to nationalism. For about one hundred years the Greek people have believed that the *raison d'être* of independent Greece was, not the welfare of her citizens, but the liberation of the much larger Irredenta beyond her borders from alien rule. This conviction, which was rooted in three thousand years of Greek history, was largely responsible for a foreign policy quite beyond the resources of the country. In the face of Turkish resistance, European antagonism and rival Balkan nationalisms, an ambitious program of territorial annexations and cultural penetration was pursued by a state whose territorial exiguousness, lack of economic self-sufficiency, and exposed geographical location made it more easily amenable to coercion than any other country in Europe. This disparity between aims and resources made for such a high degree of dependence on international developments, that for a century the course of Greek politics has been determined by the exigencies of foreign policy rather than by the correlation and clash of forces within the nation.

This generalization applies especially to the fundamental constitutional issue of the Greek state—the determination of its form of government. At first, the monarchy was accepted as the surest guarantee of viability and respectability in a militantly monarchical European society; and the value of each dynasty to the nation was primarily gauged by its effectiveness as an instrument of diplomacy. Prince Leopold of Coburg, the first serious candidate for the throne of Greece, was prompted by sound political instinct when he insisted upon an extension of boundaries as a prerequisite to his acceptance. The overthrow of King Otho, who incarnated Greek nationalism in its most romantic phase, was motivated less by popular indignation at his incorrigibly unconstitutional course than by the fact that, having forfeited the sympathy of the protecting powers, he had become a national liability. By the same token the popularity of his more hard-headed successor and of the Gluecksburg dynasty in general increased with the successes and waned with the failures of foreign policy. It ran the entire gamut of popular sentiment, from the enthusiasm that greeted King George's accession because it was accompanied by the annexation of the Ionian Islands to the anti-dynastic clamor which followed the defeat of 1897 and was exacerbated by Young Turk truculence into the Republican movement of 1909.

The paramount influence of international factors on the domestic development of Greece made it inevitable that the war of 1914, which raised the issue of national expansion more urgently and inescapably than ever before, should provoke a proportionately violent political and constitutional crisis. The first phase of this struggle between King Constantine and Premier Venizelos included the establishment of an insurgent Venizelist Government in Salonica, the expulsion of the King by the Allies, his replacement by his second son Alexander, and the triumph of Mr. Venizelos's interventionist policy. The second phase terminated with the parliamentary elections of November, 1920, when, despite the victorious outcome of the war and the rich rewards of the Treaty of Sèvres, Mr. Venizelos was decisively defeated, and by an overwhelming plebiscitary vote King Constantine was restored to the throne which had been vacated by Alexander's sudden death. A third and decisive landmark was reached in September, 1922, when the prosecution of the campaign in Anatolia after the withdrawal of Allied support led to the defeat of the Greek army, the establishment of the Plastiras-Gonatas military dictatorship, the King's definitive abdication and banishment, and the influx of more than a million refugees. Their pronounced Venizelist and anti-monarchist sentiments enabled the Republicans to cut short the reign of George II and to proclaim the Republic by a vote of a partisan assembly and ratify this action by the plebiscite of April, 1924.

The fact that the anti-monarchist movement originated in a conflict over foreign policy and triumphed as a result of military defeat is a striking demonstration of the influence of international factors on the political and constitutional development of Greece. At the same time, the establishment of the short-lived Republic of 1924-25 was the first change of regime in one hundred years that was effected without the intervention of those powers whose diplomatic and military assistance enabled Greece to achieve her independence from Ottoman rule. The legal basis for this intervention of Great Britain, France, and Russia in the internal affairs of Greece was provided by the "guarantee" attached by the three powers to the treaties which recognized the independence of the Greek state, determined its form of government, and endowed it with a dynasty. The fact that Greek independence was no sooner won than it had to be qualified by the "guarantee" of the protecting powers epitomizes, as it were, the subordination of the domestic politics of Greece to the exigencies of her international situation.

The recognition of this fact and the desire to explore its implications have determined the plan of this study. The first three chapters deal with the intellectual and institutional antecedents of constitutional government in Greece and with its development during the decade of revolution which began in the spring of 1821. Chapter IV advances the thesis that simultaneously with the attainment of independence from Ottoman rule Greece forfeited to the monarchy and to the protecting powers the internal sovereignty she had enjoyed throughout the

Insurrection. The effect of this alienation of sovereignty and especially the implications of the "guarantee" for the constitutional status of Greece are examined in the subsequent three chapters. This inquiry is mainly historical. It does not attempt to determine *a priori* the juridical meaning of the Greek "guarantee." It examines, rather, the actual policy of the "guarantor" powers on the successive occasions on which the "guarantee" was invoked, and it attempts to deduce from their behavior a pragmatic conception of this elusive diplomatic instrument and of the extent to which it impaired the sovereignty of a nominally independent state. A brief epilogue gives a summary review of Greek politics from the formal abolition of the "guarantee" in August, 1920, to the establishment of the Metaxas dictatorship and indicates some lines of further inquiry into the constitutional history of modern Greece.

The parts of this study which impinge upon the history of Greece since the outbreak of the World War of necessity touch upon certain intensely controversial topics. Needless to say, I do not presume to pass judgment on these issues. For while I was as partisan as any other Greek at the time when they were most acute, I have long since outgrown any specific bias in connection with political developments in Greece. Such lapses from objectivity as I may have been guilty of in the course of this study should therefore be put down to my general temper and outlook on politics.

Chapter One

SOURCES OF CONSTITUTIONALISM IN MODERN GREECE

I

THE PRESERVATION of Greek nationality was favored by the peculiar social and governmental system of the Ottoman Empire at the height of its power. For both the theocratic doctrines of the Sacred Law and the fiscal needs of an essentially military state dictated a status of ecclesiastical and cultural autonomy for the largest group of Christian subjects who, debarred by their religion and political subjection from governing and fighting, performed the indispensable functions of a wealth-producing and tribute-paying class. But while the peculiarities of the Ottoman system saved the Greek nation from extinction, it was not until the second half of the eighteenth century that Greek nationalism became a menace to the integrity of the Empire. Contemporaneously with and not entirely unrelated to the decay of Ottoman institutions and the definitive ebb of Ottoman conquest, both the material conditions and the collective consciousness of the subject Greeks underwent those changes which have since come to be recognized as the basic prerequisites of militant nationalism.[1] The most decisive factor in this transformation was the rise of the Greek *bourgeoisie* to a position of economic and financial dominance in the Empire and its consequent assumption of the cultural and political leadership of the Greek nation. In alliance with its traditional by-product, a mentally alert and politically restless intelligentsia, it promoted an intellectual revival which indoctrinated more

---

[1] For the decay of Ottoman institutions (feudalism, child-tribute, etc.), see John K. Kordatos, *Political History of Modern Greece*, Vol. I.

or less effectively all classes of the Greek people and prepared the national temper for decisive action.[2]

The minds of the Greek middle class and of the intelligentsia were largely formed by their contact with Western Europe during the period of intense intellectual ferment which culminated in the French Revolution. The upheaval caused by the impact of subversive ideas upon the social order of the *ancien régime* strengthened their conviction that an analogous intellectual preparation must precede the political rehabilitation of Hellenism. Influenced by the prevalent attitude of worshipful genuflexion before classical antiquity and the equally fashionable denigration of the "Low Empire," they conceived this preparation as a reorientation of the national mind from the Byzantine and ecclesiastical towards the classical tradition. Hence the numerous schools founded by wealthy Greek merchants and the more public spirited of the Phanariots and staffed by teachers educated at their expense in the West, aimed to free education from the dominance of clericalism and scholastic pedantry by introducing the study of mathematics, the natural sciences, and contemporary philosophy and by stressing the substance rather than the mere grammar of the classics. And just as they derived this essentially secular outlook and educational program from the Enlightenment, they found in the French Revolution a congenial political philosophy which could serve both as an incitement to insurrection and as the ideological foundation of the new state. The most representative of these transmitters were Adamantios Koraes, the scholar, and Rhigas of Velestinos, the man of action. Their writings, however crude and unsystematic, contain the basic political ideas in which Greek constitutionalism is grounded and are therefore an essential introduction to the constitutional history of modern Greece.

II

The main factors of the Greek intellectual revival of the late eighteenth century—mercantile wealth in the service of

[2] D. Thereianos, *Adamantios Koraes*, Introduction.

education and scholarship and the impregnation of both with the thought then prevalent in Western Europe—are strikingly exemplified in the career of Adamantios Koraes. His family, in which the pursuit of learning had been a tradition for several generations,[3] had emigrated from Chios to Smyrna, where he was born in 1748. Entering his father's firm at an early age, he was sent, in 1772, as its representative to Amsterdam. But he soon abandoned business for the study of medicine in Montpellier, whence he moved to Paris in 1788. He remained there until his death in 1833, only tepidly interested in the contemporaneous scene, because he was absorbed in what he conceived as a labor of scholarship and patriotism: the editing of the works of classical authors, which he published with the help of a regular subvention from the brothers Zosimadai, a Greek firm, of Leghorn, and periodic contributions by other Greeks of the mercantile class.

Though his direct contact with Western Europe began in the reign of Louis XV and ended in the third year of the July Monarchy, he never threw off the influences of his formative years. Having absorbed the dominant spirit of the age of reason, he concerned himself throughout his life, not with the universe and God, but with human society and man.[4] This essentially secular outlook manifested itself in his consistent anticlericalism. Applying to the Eastern Orthodox Church the criterion of social usefulness, he condemned it with Voltairean severity because by its obscurantist educational policy and its exhortations to resignation to and acquiescence in Ottoman rule on the ground of the divine origin of all authority, it retarded the intellectual progress and the political liberation of the Greek nation.[5] At the same time, he shared the prevalent contemporary faith in human perfectibility through the ability of reason to convert knowledge into both virtue and power, and

[3] His paternal grandfather, Antonios Koraes, was one of the leaders of the educational movement early in the eighteenth century.
[4] He also kept up a voluminous and far-flung correspondence and translated Beccaria's *Crimes and Punishment*.
[5] Thereianos, *op. cit.*, I, 42.

he therefore regarded education as the prime molder of human destiny. The result of these convictions was his lifelong effort to lay the groundwork of a system of secular and utilitarian education which should inspire the Greek people with the will to freedom and equip them for the good life as a free nation. This effort was directed into two main channels: reform of the language, intended to provide a common literary medium as a prerequisite to political unity;[6] and familiarization of his countrymen with the thought of their ancestors through the publication of a monumental series of the Greek classics. The extensive prolegomena to these successive editions, and particularly to Aristotle's *Politics,* which appeared six months after the outbreak of the Greek War of Independence, contain the most coherent exposition of his political philosophy.[7]

Koraes was by no means an idolatrous worshiper of the ancients. He contrasted the elevation and wisdom of their thinking in the fields of ethics and politics with the ineptitude of their statecraft; but being essentially a moralist, he overlooked the environmental causes of this discrepancy between thought and action and was inclined to attribute the failure of the Greeks to achieve political unity to their faults of character, of which he considered envy the worst because it bred injustice and dissension. Since he detected the same shortcomings in the modern Greeks, he had grave misgivings about their ability to live in peace and unity after the attainment of independence. But true to his perfectibilist faith, he was convinced that these defects, which he believed had been aggravated by centuries of subjection to Turkish rule, could be remedied by education. With the naïveté of the cloistered theorist, he ascribed the

---

[6] He sought to effect a compromise between the "Atticists," who wanted to restore classical Greek, and the advocates of the spoken tongue as a literary medium. By purging the vernacular of post-classical accretions and by adapting it to ancient grammatical forms, he created the "Katharevoussa," which became the official, but never the spoken or the literary, language of modern Greece. Its gradual amalgamation with the spoken idiom has produced the mixed language of the educated classes which is becoming increasingly prevalent and seems to promise a solution of bilingualism.

[7] Adamantios Koraes, ed., *Prolegomena to the Politics of Aristotle.*

internecine strife which attended the War of Independence to the intellectual and moral unpreparedness of his countrymen; and he would, therefore, have preferred to postpone the Insurrection until the middle of the nineteenth century in order to allow the educational effort begun in his generation to bear fruit.

With this predisposition to stress the human factor[8] in social change, he combined a rather uncritical acceptance of the Natural Rights school of political thought. He adopted the hypothesis of a pre-social state of nature and the contractual origin of society, and borrowed from all three of its main variants, apparently unaware of their contradictions. Hobbes, Locke, and Rousseau jostle one another in attempts at political theorizing such as the statement that "men were united to form civil society in order to escape the daily conflicts and the injustice resulting from the untempered freedom prevalent in a state of nature"; the assertion that when they effected this union "they gave up only a small part of their unlimited freedom in order to preserve the rest in peace"; the definition of liberty as "the authority enjoyed by every citizen to do everything not forbidden by the law, which means, not whatever he will, but what he willed when he first joined his fellow citizens to form a political society"; and the definition of law as "the expression of the general will of a group of men" who, in order to set up a state, "have bound themselves by means of a political compact."[9] With regard to equality, he held that "though nature has endowed us at birth with identical senses, passions, and needs," the postnatal development of every individual diverges more and more from that of his fellows. He described the resultant inequality as "born of necessity" and "nature's handiwork," and he concluded, citing Aristotle, that the only permanent equality is founded on merit.[10] He warned that equality

---

[8] "It is a misfortune that we have revolted at a time when public education had hardly begun." Koraes to Jefferson, July 10, 1823. Manuscript in U. S. Department of State, Washington, D. C. Letters to Jefferson, Series 2, Vol. XXII, No. 109. See also F. Argyropoulos, *Adamantios Koraes*, p. 168.

[9] Koraes, *op. cit.*   [10] *Ibid.*

before the law (*isonomia*) must not be confused with equality of status (*isotimia*); and in a somewhat ambiguous passage, which seems to hark back to Sieyès's classic distinction between active and passive citizens, he maintained that in all "legally constituted states there must be both those who govern and those who are governed, those who contribute the funds needed for public expenditure and those who allocate these contributions."[11]

These theoretical views, applied to the realities of Greek politics, explain Koraes's hostility to the hereditary aristocracy which had developed in the Ionian Islands under Venetian rule, his distrust of the landowning oligarchy of Greece proper, and his contempt for the Phanariots, who were doubly odious to him as claimants of the Byzantine heritage and as servants of the Ottoman Government. But though his love of democracy and equality often betrayed him into pedantic vagaries, he was on solid ground when he strongly deprecated the selection of a dynasty from the native aristocracy of Greece. For this opinion did not merely reflect his anti-aristocratic prejudices but also was based on a shrewd appraisal of the egalitarian temper of a people singularly averse to elevating one of themselves to a position of unique eminence, which thereby becomes inaccessible to the rest.[12]

Koraes's opinions become increasingly moderate as he proceeds from generalities to specific prescriptions. The more radical phases of the French Revolution must have bred in him a fear of democracy, "the polity of the foolish," which he rejects as decisively as he rejects oligarchy, "the polity of the cunning." His reiterated advice to his insurgent countrymen is that they follow "the middle road."[13] The lawmakers must be selected by and among the most "sagacious" citizens. "And since these men of sagacity are to be found neither among the very rich nor among the excessively poor, the majority of the legislators should be recruited from the middle class," which, he characteristically adds, "is the most easily amenable to reason."[14] He

[11] *Ibid.*   [12] *Ibid.*   [13] *Ibid.*   [14] *Ibid.*

conceives the aim of "good legislation" to be the welfare of the majority; and he dismisses the troublesome problem of the rights of the minority with the sanguine assertion that "whatever is for the good of the many cannot be detrimental to any of the few."[15] Though convinced that "man is an acquisitive, just as he is a political, animal and that he would never have become civilized without the institution of private property," he deprecated the accumulation of wealth and believed that, given the absence of both an aristocracy on the West-European pattern and a plutocracy and the preponderance of people of moderate means, Greece had a sound social basis for what he considered a sensible form of government. He capped this Jeffersonian doctrine, appropriately enough, with a panegyric of agriculture, the source of prosperity and the breeder of "virtue," to which he therefore urged his countrymen to devote themselves even before they engaged in "commerce and the arts," in order to repair the material and spiritual ravages of the Insurrection.[16]

With regard to the form of government to be adopted by the new state, Koraes either wavered between his theoretical preferences and what he conceived to be the exigencies of the international position of Greece or refrained from detailed prescription, possibly because he did not feel at home in the field of constitutional theory. The only settled convictions discernible in his writings are a strong aversion to absolutism and a dauntless faith in constitutional and representative government. Though he was apparently not opposed to monarchy on principle and, indeed, regarded it as a necessity for "populous and large states," he deemed it an expensive luxury for a small and poor country and asserted that "subjection to a king" would be tantamount to "a second conquest."[17] But realizing that

[15] *Ibid.*   [16] *Ibid.*
[17] Compare Lombardos' speech, Feb. 25, 1874 (addressing the King): "Monarchy has none of the reasons for existence obtaining in the rest of Europe. Nevertheless, you will remain stable if you understand this, we are all republicans, and we also love equality more than liberty. And we don't recognize any Greek as above the rest of us. Hence a republic is impossible for the present." Cited by G. Philaretos, *Notes, 1848–1923.*

post-Napoleonic Europe would hardly tolerate both an independent and a republican Greece, he conceded the advisability of establishing a monarchial form of government, provided it was limited by a constitution patterned after the French Charter of 1814 and the Greek people had a voice in the selection of their first ruler. At the same time, on the not unreasonable assumption that once this selection was made Greece would be committed to the power or group of powers most closely related to her dynasty and estranged from the rest, he urged the expediency of delay in the hope that "as long as they remain without a king, the Greeks will have all the Christian monarchs for their protectors."[18]

Disappointed in this hope and disillusioned with Europe, he turned, two years later, to Jefferson with a request for his expert advice. He was rewarded with a dissertation in the happiest Jeffersonian vein "on the subject of national government," in which the veteran theorist and statesman commended the Greeks for having begun "at the right end," that is, with education, and, after stressing the relativity of political systems and declaring that the governmental principles of Athens and Lacedaemon "are not the doctrines of the present age," proceeded to expound federalism and states' rights, the system of checks and balances, the advantages and dangers of a bicameral legislature, the difference between the collegiate and a single executive, the importance of providing for amendment of the constitution, and the need of incorporating in it a Bill of Rights for the "protection of the life, liberty, property and safety of the citizen." As regards the basic form of government, while insisting on a single in preference to a collegiate executive, he left the question whether this "ethnarch" should be elective or "more stable" and "his office more permanent" to be deter-

---

[18] "It is a misfortune for us," he writes to Jefferson, July 10, 1823, obviously referring to the post-Napoleonic reaction, "that we are the neighbors of self-styled enlightened nations at a time when they are passing through a crisis; and even if this crisis terminates in the triumph of the little freedom they are enjoying, we may fear that they will grant liberty to Greece only in so far as it is compatible with their interests." Manuscript in U. S. Department of State, Washington, D. C. Letters to Jefferson, Series 2, Vol. XXII, No. 109.

mined by the position of Greece "among the warring powers of Europe." Finally, he recommended a unitary rather than a federal state as more suitable to the probable size of Greece, and strict adherence to representative government, a device which gives modern peoples a "signal advantage" over the ancients.[19] These views were the more acceptable to Koraes because they supported his own conviction that the reasons for the downfall of ancient Greece, apart from the faults and vices of the people, were the territorial and political disunion of the city states and the direct participation of the citizens in government.[20] It was obviously with Jefferson's reservations regarding federalism and his advice about representative institutions in mind that he urged Mavrocordatos "to do all in his power to organize the new Greek state on the Anglo-American pattern."

Deeply distressed by the domestic strife that attended the Insurrection almost from its inception, he at first greeted Capodistrias as a liberator, comparable to Timoleon of Syracuse, who would put an end to factionalism and anarchy and salvage the hard-won independence of Greece. But, as was to be expected from a doctrinaire liberal who surveyed the situation from his ivory tower in distant Paris, he soon joined the ranks of the president's enemies and accused him of having "abolished the Constitution, united the three separate powers of the State in his own person and . . . dared to smash the most effective weapon of liberty—freedom of the press." At the same time, inveterately Russophobe even after Russia's decisive contribution to the independence of Greece, he accepted uncritically the theory of Capodistrias's subserviency to Russia and laid the ultimate blame for his assassination at the door of the Holy Alliance, "which sent him to subjugate Greece to the Russian yoke."[21]

With a corresponding revival of his lifelong faith in the

---

[19] Jefferson to Koraes, Oct. 31, 1823. H. A. Washington, ed., *Writings of Thomas Jefferson*, VII, 318–24.

[20] "The more similar the Constitution of Greece is to yours, the more your interests will be favored in preference to those of other countries." Koraes to Jefferson, Jan. 20, 1825.   [21] John Mavrogordato, *Modern Greece*, p. 12.

relative disinterestedness of France, after the passing of Capodistrias Koraes urged that Greece should place herself under French protection and reorganize her governmental system under French guidance. As to the nature of this system, he apparently no longer felt compelled to sacrifice his republican sympathies to international exigencies: a king would be "the worst thing for Greece even if he were the equal of Marcus Aurelius." Characteristic of this last phase, during which he clung to the ideals of a lifetime with the querulous tenacity of old age, was the opinion, expressed apropos of King Otho's designation by the powers, that Greece would be far better off with Lafayette as a "guide" than with a mere "kinglet of eighteen" as a ruler. This preference for the statesman who carried the libertarian tradition of 1789 down to the reign of Louis Philippe came very fittingly from this contemporary scholar who, himself a survival of the Enlightenment and the Revolution, had been throughout a long life their foremost interpreter to renascent Greece.

III

Vastly different were the personality and the career of Rhigas of Velestinos, a contemporary of Koraes and, like him, a product and a leader of the intellectual preparation that preceded the Greek War of Independence. His brief but chequered life and the manner of his death stamp him as a combination of dreamer and man of action, bent upon the immediate achievement of independence and hence inclined to the short-cuts of agitation and conspiracy rather than the slow processes of education as a prelude to insurrection.[22] The indictment of his Austrian captors, who handed him over to the Ottoman authorities to be executed (June 12, 1798), accused him of conspiring "to bring about an uprising of the Greek nation ... against its legitimate ruler and to establish a popular government patterned on the French Constitution."[23] While this is

[22] Born in 1757. Arrested by the Austrian police in Trieste, Dec. 19, 1797; handed over to the Turkish authorities and executed (probably) during the night of June 11-12, 1798.

[23] Report of Vienna police to the Minister of the Interior, Dec. 28, 1797.

an accurate description of his immediate aim, a study of his most effective writings, the revolutionary battle hymn and his *Constitution,* discloses a political program of much larger scope: the reconstruction of the Ottoman Empire into a democratic commonwealth embracing all races and creeds and founded upon political liberty and social justice. That Rhigas was not a narrow nationalist, but a generous-hearted humanitarian who abhorred oppression irrespective of its racial or class incidence, no student of his life and of his writings can doubt. But as a widely traveled observer, a keen student of Balkan conditions, and an experienced diplomat trained in the Phanariot chancelleries of the Danubian principalities, he must have known that his dazzling vision of a revolution which was to be at once political, social, and supernational could not, in the prevailing circumstances, be translated into a program of action. For it postulated a basic cultural unity, similar to that enjoyed by France for centuries before her Revolution, which was notoriously lacking both in the Ottoman Empire as a whole and among its Christian subjects; it presupposed the acceptance of Greek leadership, which was by no means certain, despite the as yet embryonic condition of the other Balkan nationalisms at the end of the eighteenth century; and it assumed an attitude of aloofness and acquiescence, if not of active support, on the part of the European powers, which was equally problematic. Nor could Rhigas have been unaware of the inconsistencies and contradictions of his revolutionary gospel. Though he intended it for all the peoples of the Empire, "Christians and Turks" without distinction of religion, "for all are the children of God and descendants of Adam,"[24] he preached it in the name of the Cross and made St. Sophia its symbol and its goal. Even if he had confined it to the Sultan's Christian subjects, the effectiveness of its appeal was impaired by the fact that it was couched in the Greek language, was largely inspired by Greek history, and voiced essentially Greek aspirations.

It is therefore apparent that Rhigas adopted in his hortatory

[24] Konstantinos Amantos, *Documents concerning Rhigas of Velestinos,* p. 29.

writings the time-honored technique of revolutionary agitation. While his vision of universal brotherhood within a regenerated Ottoman Empire was no less sincere than Mazzini's dream of a European union of free peoples, he had, like the great apostle of Italian unity, a more immediate and pressing aim: the restoration of Hellenism to its political independence and primacy. This was the program of Rhigas the statesman. But since all existing discontents are fish to an agitator's net, Rhigas the agitator addressed his impassioned revolutionary call to all the incipient separatism within the Empire, firmly convinced, like all the prophets of romantic and liberal nationalism, that universal brotherhood would inevitably result from the liberation of his own nation. Nor were his efforts entirely wasted, for his revolutionary gospel let into the Balkan peninsula the new winds of doctrine blowing from the West and to that extent sowed the seed of future change. At the same time, within the narrower field of his immediate endeavor, his precept and example created a legend which contributed potently to the growth of the militant national consciousness that launched the War of Independence a generation after his death.[25]

It is evident from the map (significantly surmounted with a picture of Alexander the Great), which Rhigas circulated "for the enlightenment of the nation," that he intended the territorial extent of the new state to conform to the extreme historical claims of Hellenism. On the other hand, he patterned its public law and political institutions upon those of Revolutionary France. His *New Polity of the People of Rumeli, Asia Minor, the Mediterranean Islands and Wallacho-Moldavia*,[26] while revealing the author's familiarity with most of the constitutional literature of the Revolution, is largely borrowed from the democratic and republican Constitution of the Year I. It begins with an explanation of the origin of society, and the

---

[25] Rhigas's "Battle Hymn."
[26] He was private secretary to successive Phanariot governors of Moldavia and Wallachia and was engaged because of his French and republican sympathies as "dragoman" of the French consulate in Wallachia. See Phanis Michalopoulos, *Rhigas of Velestinos*.

state, which is a popularized and somewhat fanciful mixture of Rousseau, Hobbes, and the Natural Rights theory. He attributes the abandonment of the state of nature and the founding of civil society to the desire of men to safeguard their natural rights, "of which no one on earth may deprive them," and which are equality before the law, liberty, and security. The ensuing *Declaration of the Rights of Man,* being an instrument of propaganda addressed to a heterogeneous and variously oppressed constituency, is more diffuse and explanatory and at the same time more broadly humanitarian than its French prototype. Thus, it does not mention private property among the natural rights, but recognizes it implicitly by including it in the concept of security and by prohibiting expropriation except in case of public need and after due indemnification. On the other hand, the provision (apparently borrowed from Byzantine law and the *seisachtheia* of the Greek city states) [27] authorizing cancellation of all debts after a five-year period during which the creditor has received the equivalent of his principal in interest, shows little respect for property rights and the letter of contractual obligations.[28] Further, the *Declaration* significantly stresses the absence of religious discrimination as part of the concept of equality, defines law as "a free decision made with the consent of the entire people," and prohibits its retroactive application, grants the franchise to "the mass of the people" (and not merely to "the rich and the notables"), guarantees freedom of speech, of the press, and of assembly, lays down the principle of universal, compulsory, and free education, provides for due process of law, rejects summary execution even in cases involving conspiracy against the state, and proclaims the right and duty of resistance to oppression.

[27] Fustel de Coulanges thinks it applied to the freeing of clients from the eupatrids (enabling them to own land). "Ceux qui sur cette terre subissaiont la cruelle servitude et tremblaient devant un maitre, je les ai faits libres." *La Cité antique,* p. 316.

[28] Th. Tsatsos, "Notes on Rhigas's 'Polity,'" in Amantos, *op. cit.* Mr. Tsatsos infers from this provision, which points to an extremely high rate of interest, the great scarcity of liquid money in Greece toward the end of the eighteenth century.

The *Constitution* proper, by declaring "a Greek and a citizen" any one who speaks the vernacular "even if he resides in the Antipodes," subscribes to one of the basic ideas of Greek nationalism, the unity of the Greek people irrespective of territorial boundaries.[29] It also recognizes the cultural dependence of the new state on its more enlightened Western neighbors by conferring citizenship and special honors on Europeans who transplant to Greece the "wisdom and the arts" of the West. For the rest, it follows faithfully the Constitution of the Year I, except in the provisions for a bicameral legislature and a collegiate executive of five members, which are adapted, with slight variations, from the Constitution of the Year III.

This eclectic borrowing, necessitated by Rhigas's lack of originality as a political thinker, was also dictated by his aims. His self-imposed task was not to draw up the fundamental law of a state that was yet to be born, but to hasten its birth by his propagandist writings. It was with a view to increasing the efficacy of his call to national insurrection that he attempted to formulate the principles of natural rights, popular sovereignty, representative government, and the unitary state, which were basic to the constitutional development of modern Greece.[30]

IV

Quite independently of the educational work of Koraes and the revolutionary agitation of Rhigas, the ideas of the French Revolution, having made their way at the turn of the

[29] Rhigas's preference for the spoken tongue, which he uses to the best of his ability in his writings, is characteristic of his democratic temper, his skill as an agitator, and his wisdom as a statesman.

[30] It can hardly be maintained, however, that Rhigas's constitution exerted much direct influence on the Greek Revolution. For though Rhigas's constitution was doubtless known to his contemporaries and seems to have inspired *The Greek Monarchy*, written by John Kolettes in 1806 and dedicated to Rhigas, it cannot have had a very wide circulation during the following generation, because it was among the documents confiscated by the Austrian police at the time of his arrest. The text I have used was first published by P. Chiotis in 1871 in the Greek periodical *Parthenon* and was reissued in pamphlet form in 1924. On the other hand, the Preamble was much more widely known, having been circulated as part of Rhigas's "Battle Hymn." For a detailed discussion of Rhigas's writings see Amantos, *op. cit.*, Introduction.

century to the westernmost region of Greece in the wake of the French armies, brought about social and political changes, the repercussions of which were eventually felt by the entire nation. The Ionian Islands (otherwise called Heptanesus on account of their number), have played an important part in the history of medieval and modern Greece. Their location made them a bridge for the cultural traffic which flowed mostly from East to West in the heyday of the Byzantine Empire but reversed itself after the Latin and the Ottoman conquests. Enjoying among the regions of Greece the unique distinction of freedom from Ottoman rule, they developed in the course of their long contact with the West a culture which, except for their firm adherence to the Eastern Orthodox Church, was largely derived from Italy. During four centuries of political association with Venice,[31] they built up a tradition of strictly conditional and oligarchic but effective self-government functioning in a society which was structurally akin to the classic pattern of the *ancien régime* and politically dominated by a small and proud aristocracy.[32] Relatively untouched by the conservative influences emanating from distant Constantinople and in close contact with the educational revival and linguistic reform carried out in the cities of the nearby Epirotic mainland, they initiated early in the nineteenth century the most original and creative literary movement in modern Greece, and thereby helped to establish the spoken tongue as the dominant medium of modern Greek literature. Finally, their proximity to the West, their political vicissitudes from the end of Venetian rule in 1797 to the union with Greece in 1864, and the structure of their society, which included, besides a masterful aristocracy, a wide-awake and militant *bourgeoisie* and intelligentsia and a far from supine artisan class and peasantry, made them a laboratory of political experimentation and a school of leadership for the entire nation. It was during the troubled period following

[31] 1386–1797.
[32] Of the four major islands, Corfu (the capital) and Zanta were most aristocratic, the number of families entered in the latter's Golden Book being only ninety-three; whereas Kephallonia and Santa Maura were more democratic.

the French incursion into the Heptanesian archipelago that John Capodistrias, a native of Corfu, won his spurs in diplomacy and statesmanship. While serving under the French, Russian, and British armies of occupation, Theodore Colocotronis and other free lances from the mainland lost some of their uncritical admiration for European omniscience and omnipotence and gained an insight into European diplomacy which convinced them that the liberation of Greece could not be achieved by the favor of this or that power, but through the self-reliant and resolute exertions of the Greek people. The encouragement of education under British rule, in conjunction with the long fight against the British protectorate, produced an intelligent and politically-minded citizenry whose representatives in the Greek Parliament after the union brought considerable intellectual distinction into Greek politics. The extent and variety of their influence can be gauged by the fact that they included men as different in outlook as George Theotokis, the most aristocratic of Greek prime ministers, Constantine Lombardos, whose liberal constitutionalism did not always conceal his republican convictions, and Roccos Hoidas, one of the two consistent Republicans to enter the Greek Parliament before 1909 and a good deal of a socialist as well.

The impact of French ideas upon the Islands produced political convulsions analogous to those in other parts of Europe where the revolutionary armies had carried the explosive trinity of liberty, equality, and fraternity. Until the coming of the French, the Heptanesian archipelago had formed a vestigial part of the Venetian Empire, but it had enjoyed a large degree of autonomy under the rule of the local aristocracy. The *Signoria* of Venice contented itself with the exercise of general and supreme control through its appointed agents: a governor general, with a three-year term, a governor for each of the islands, a grand judge, and three "inquisitors" sent out periodically to investigate conditions and report on the conduct of all public officials. The actual rulers were the Heptanesian aristocracy, registered in a Golden Book like its Venetian proto-

SOURCES OF CONSTITUTIONALISM

type, and acting through its representatives who constituted the Grand Council. This body, meeting annually, elected and delegated its powers to "little councils" for each of the Islands; and these in turn discharged their functions through two elective bodies: (*a*) the syndics—a collegiate mayoralty—, and (*b*) the judges, who assisted the grand judge in a consultative capacity. Apart from these permanent organs, the Islands had direct access to the home government through special emissaries who could be sent whenever necessary to present grievances.

This oligarchic regime was brought to an end when the Islands were occupied by a detachment of Bonaparte's troops after his first Italian campaign and the preliminaries of Loeben. Though the French occupation lasted less than two years, it brought about a decisive transformation in the temper and considerable change in the institutions of the Heptanesian people. The overthrow of the oligarchic government, the burning of the Golden Book, Bonaparte's proclamation from Milan decreeing the abolition of feudalism,[33] the democratization of the municipal bodies, the freeing of the peasantry from compulsory labor in the government salt works, the reform of civil and criminal justice, and the extension of educational facilities released popular forces which would henceforth have to be reckoned with regardless of the political regime or the international status of the Islands. The attempt made by the oligarchs after the French had been driven out by the Russians to restore government by the *principali e notabili* provoked popular uprisings against what was characteristically dubbed the "Byzantine Constitution." Following the departure of the Russian troops this democratic temper found expression in the stillborn Constitution of 1801, which proclaimed in its preamble that natural rights confer "perfect equality" and hence "the equal right to participate in making the social contract and the laws required for its functioning, and to elect representatives to whom the totality of citizens delegate their power." Somewhat less daring in its provisions, it combined universal suffrage with

[33] Seventh Brumaire, Sixth Year of the Republic; not immediately enforced.

indirect election and made eligibility to the "Executive Council" a privilege of only the "best citizens" (*aristoi*), that is, landowners who had reached their thirtieth year:—a restriction apparently intended to conciliate the aristocracy and showing that its long rule had bred in the Heptanesian people a deferential and trusting attitude toward their "betters."

Owing to the opposition of the conservatives, these provisions remained a dead letter until the change in the international status of the Islands brought about by the Treaty of Amiens necessitated a new constitutional deal. The ensuing Constitution of 1803 was a rather conservative bourgeois document cast to large extent in the institutional molds of the Venetian regime. It created a more elastic electorate based, not on hereditary privilege, but on individual—mainly property—qualifications. At the same time, it showed a distinctly egalitarian bias by disfranchising bachelors under sixty in order to discourage celibacy as a means of averting the parceling out of property. Under its provisions the assembly of each island, composed of the active citizens and meeting every two years, elected its quota of representatives to the Heptanesian Parliament, which consisted of a lower House and a Senate with a membership of forty and seventeen, respectively. The former, during its annual session of two months, elected the President of the Republic, the seven members of the supreme court, the chiefs of the administrative departments, and the auditors. The Senate, on the other hand, of whose membership half were re-elected annually, functioned as the executive branch of the government and was therefore presided over by the President of the Republic. Both the chief executive and the Senate were under surveillance of the auditors and subject to impeachment by the lower house. Finally, a judiciary was set up independent of both the executive and the legislature; ability to read and write Greek, which had been officially banned under Venetian rule, was made a requirement for holding public office, and a process of revision was devised for several Articles designated as "non-essential."

This constitution of the first independent Greek state since the fall of Constantinople, in the drafting of which the youthful John Capodistrias took a prominent part as secretary of state, secured for the Islands a period of orderly and peaceful self-government until their reoccupation by French troops under Marshal Berthier in accordance with the Tilsit agreements put an end to Heptanesian independence and closed a decade of intensive constitutional experimentation. Reconquered by the British in 1814 and converted (by the Treaty of November 5, 1815) into a British protectorate, "the United States of the Ionian Islands" were compelled to observe an official neutrality during the War of Independence and to wait until 1864 for their union with Greece. Though they kept up increasingly close economic and cultural relations with Greece throughout this period and indirectly exerted considerable political influence, they were obviously unable to give the new state during its turbulent formative years the full benefit of their recent experiments with political institutions.

V

While familiarity with the political thought of the West was confined at the outbreak of the War of Independence to a very small educated minority, the bulk of the Greek people were not entirely unpracticed in the rudimentary processes of self-government. They owed this training to the large measure of autonomy they enjoyed under Ottoman rule.[34] This regime, which was fostered by the peculiar predilection of the theocratic Ottoman state for dealing with its non-Moslem subjects as corporate units rather than as individuals, had two aspects: fundamentally ecclesiastical and communal, it embraced the entire "Romaic Nation," that is, the Christian subjects of the Sultan who belonged to the Eastern Orthodox Church; at the same time, in the preponderantly Greek regions of the Empire, it assumed a territorial character and developed concurrently into municipal and provincial self-government.

Because it was granted by a theocratic state, the autonomous

[34] N. G. Moschovakis, *Public Law in Greece under Turkish Rule*.

status of the "Romaic Nation" was itself a theocracy. The Patriarch of Constantinople was not merely the religious head of the Eastern Orthodox community but also, subject to the ultimate control of the Imperial Government, its political chief. By virtue of his spiritual authority he was vested with far-reaching temporal powers—judicial, fiscal, and administrative, which were delegated to the ecclesiastical hierarchy, from archbishops down to village priests, and were exercised with the coöperation of elected lay councils.[35] The erection within the framework of the Empire of this autonomous entity which was coterminous with the Greek Church, enabled a Mohammedan state to stand aloof from the governance of those of its subjects who were outside the ambit of the Sacred Law and, at the same time, to secure their allegiance by transferring responsibility for their good behavior to the shoulders of their ecclesiastical and lay leaders. The latter were enjoined, in the words of Sultan Mahmud II, "to watch day and night over those entrusted to their guidance, to observe their conduct and to discover and report their lawless actions to my government"; in short, to be the agents of the paramount power in perpetuating the subjection of their flock. The execution of Patriarch Gregory V with several prelates and lay dignitaries in April, 1821, because of their failure to avert the outbreak of the Greek Insurrection is a classic illustration of the manner—both preventive and repressive—in which this system of government by hostages was intended to function and accounts for the political conservatism of the Greek Church quite as much as its inherently authoritarian and anti-revolutionary bias.[36]

The same principle of corporate relationship between rulers and ruled was applied by the Ottoman Empire to the fiscal obligations of its Greek subjects; but the burden of collective responsibility was shifted from the Church, which represented the "Romaic Nation" in its entirety, to its component units, that is, the autonomous communes. Hence, the regime of municipal

---

[35] *Ibid.*, pp. 62–64.
[36] See S. Tricoupes, *History of the Greek Revolution*, Vol. II.

autonomy, which existed in most parts of Greece during the Frankish and Byzantine periods, was maintained and expanded after the Ottoman conquest, because it not only fitted into the Ottoman system of indirect government but also served the peculiar needs of fiscal administration. These arose basically from the prevalent method of raising revenue, whereby the contribution of each province to the imperial treasury was fixed in advance and the task of collection was turned over to the provincial authorities, who in turn found it expedient to invoke the coöperation of the representatives of the subject race in order to distribute the quota among districts and communes and transfer to them responsibility for full payment. This procedure was acceptable both to the Ottoman authorities, because it concentrated responsibility and facilitated the exertion of pressure, and to the Greek taxpayers because it reduced contact with Ottoman officials to a minimum and promoted self-government. Thus, in the preponderantly Greek parts of the Empire the commune functioned not merely as a component unit of the "Romaic Nation" governed by its lay elders and the clergy in accordance with the privileged status conferred upon the Greek Church but also as a full-fledged municipality having complete charge of its internal administration and as a buffer between its individual members and the organs of the central government.

Upon this substructure of municipal self-government was superimposed a regime of provincial autonomy which, dictated as it was by strategic, economic, and often purely personal considerations, varied enormously from one region to another and was repeatedly modified by the changing exigencies of imperial policy. Thus the dour and inaccessible region of Maina enjoyed virtual independence under the most tenuous form of Ottoman suzerainty, symbolized by a nominal tribute; and even after the abortive insurrection of 1770, except for the appointment of its headman by the Admiral of the Fleet (Capoudan Pasha), and the raising of the tribute from four to fifteen thousand *piastres,* it retained intact its peculiar social organization and its institutions of self-government. The Aegean Islands, which were held much more firmly within the imperial framework because of their economic and strategic importance, were governed by their native oligarchies of "primates"; and though the Admiral of the Fleet, who represented the central government in the great majority of the Islands, could oppose his veto to all the decisions of the local authorities and had exclusive jurisdiction in the field of criminal justice, he generally refrained from interference as long as they were not in arrears with their taxes, kept the peace, and did not attempt to sever their connection with the Empire. Continental Greece, on the other hand, which was largely rural and pastoral and in its mountainous sections a hotbed of chronic insurgency, was under the direct control of the Imperial Government except for a few isolated regions, the most remarkable of which were two federations of industrial and commercial communities in Eastern Thessaly. Finally, the Peloponnesus, after the Venetians had been driven out in the first quarter of the eighteenth century, was placed under an elaborate hierarchy of Ottoman officials; but having at the same time retained and expanded its autonomous institutions, it presented on the eve of the Insurrection the clearest pattern of their relation to and co-ordination with the central government.[37]

The main functionaries of the Imperial Government in the Peloponnesus were the Governor General, a Governor (*Voivod*), mainly concerned with the collection of taxes, a judge (*Kadi*), a treasurer, and a chief constable for each of the twenty-four districts. But they were by no means the sole or the absolute rulers of the province. They were aided, checked and sometimes overridden by the representatives of the local population, Moslem and Christian, with the latter—the so-called "headmen" or primates (*kodjabashis*)[38] of each district—playing by far the more influential role both as spokesmen for the much larger constituency and as the lay leaders of a com-

---

[37] For a description of Provincial autonomy see A. Mamoukas, *Documents Relating to the Greek Renaissance*, Vol. XI.

[38] On the powers of the *kodjabashis* see Mamoukas, *op. cit.*, pp. 314–15.

pact fragment of the "Romaic Nation." Elected annually by the elders (*demogeronts*) of the communes, the primates were the intermediaries between their constituents and the paramount power. Though two of them, "the most powerful," sat permanently on the Executive Council of the Governor General, he convoked the entire group annually as an advisory body in order to deliberate with them concerning the needs of the province, draw up its internal budget, fix the amount of its contribution to the imperial treasury, and distribute the burden among the districts. The second step in the devolution of functions and responsibility was the transmission of these decisions to the regular annual meetings of the district assembly, composed of the elders of the communes, which, under the presidency of the *Voivod*, reviewed the administration of the outgoing primates, elected their successors, and after adding to the estimates of the domestic needs of the district its share of the imperial tax load, apportioned the total among the communes. Finally, the task of raising the sum allotted to each commune devolved upon the elders, who, after making an estimate of municipal expenditures assessed the individual taxpayer for both according to their capacity.

Concomitant with the responsibility borne by the elected representatives of the subject race, was commensurate influence and power.

The primates had the right to arbitrate and even to try all cases of whatever nature between *rayas* (non-Moslems), and no Turkish official could intervene if both litigants were satisfied with the decision. No distribution of the tax load or the collection of the taxes could be effected without their authorization and advice. It was through them that all petitions of the towns and villages were transmitted to the Turkish authorities. Even when imprisoned, Christians could resort to them in order to regain their freedom.

In short, under normal conditions, they wielded greater power than the *Voivod* and the other officials of the central government. Conflicts arising between the two parallel authorities were as a rule threshed out before the district assembly, which, if necessary, convened in extraordinary session. And only in case of failure to reach settlement was the question at issue carried to the Governor General for adjudication. But though "they were accountable to him only for their stewardship and he alone had the right to mete out to them rewards or punishments," even his decisions were not final. For the Peloponnesus shared with Chios the privilege of maintaining in Constantinople resident ambassadors who assiduously cultivated the favor of the mighty and, though often more concerned with their personal interests than with the welfare of their constituents, were able because of their proximity to the source of power to secure the redress of grievances and curb the arbitrary velleities of provincial officials.

Though they held office by election and during good behavior and were subject to removal by the Governor General, the representatives of the subject Greeks inevitably developed into a ruling class. In the first place, the primates were elected indirectly by the elders of the commune, who in turn were chosen by acclamation, that is, without the safeguards of secrecy, by a more or less limited number of voters. But more than the franchise, which was far from uniform, and electoral procedure, the very nature of the office tended to confine eligibility to the "most prominent with respect to wealth and influence." Enlightened self-interest dictated that those who were responsible for the fiscal obligations of the community should be recruited among its wealthiest members. And since in the last analysis they functioned as mediators and intercessors on behalf of a subject race rather than as representatives of a free people, their effectiveness was increased by the prolongation of their tenure (through re-election or confirmation by the Governor General), which enabled them to strengthen their ascendancy over the Ottoman authorities. Nor were the Peloponnesian landowners, from whom the primates were mainly drawn, reluctant to accept a position of responsibility which they could use for the furtherance of their economic interests. On the other hand, though essentially imbued with the mentality of a possessing class and often inclined to be haughty and oppressive toward those whom they were elected to protect, the egalitarian attitude of the Ottoman Empire toward its Christian subjects reduced their civil status to the level of their lowliest co-religionists. Their economic interests and the exercise of power may have induced in them a feeling of closer affinity with the corresponding class of the ruling race. But, as the Insurrection of 1821 was to prove conclusively, solidarity with their fellow Christians and responsibility for their conduct was thrust upon them by the fundamental law of a theocratic state which recognized religion only as the decisive line of cleavage among its subjects.

Thanks to this regime, which at its best enabled two parallel authorities to function concurrently by consultation and adjustment, the Greek people were acquainted with the underlying assumptions and the mechanics of representative government and were able to set up, during the War of Independence, the rudiments of political and administrative organization. At the same time, the domestic struggle which arose from sectional and economic differences and was aggravated by personal passions, would probably have been less violent if the insurgent Greeks had not been made politically minded by the long practice of conditional self-government under Ottoman rule. And though this ceaseless preoccupation with politics obstructed the progress of the Revolution and endangered its outcome, it contributed powerfully to the building of a libertarian and constitutionalist tradition. For a closer view of this tradition we must now turn to the constitutional experiments of the Revolution.

Chapter Two

THE CONSTITUTIONS OF THE REVOLUTION

I

THE INITIAL SUCCESSES of the Greek insurgents in the Peloponnesus, the Aegean Islands, and continental Greece confronted them with the urgent task of setting up a new government which would fill the void left by the overthrow of Ottoman rule and undertake the military and diplomatic conduct of the prospective struggle. The nature of this government was determined by (*a*) the exigencies of the international situation, (*b*) the social forces and the shifting political alignments of insurgent Greece, and (*c*) the revolutionary ideas and the exemplars of representative institutions imported from Western Europe. Because the constitutions of the Greek Revolution reflected most obviously, in their borrowed concepts and terminology, the third of these factors, they have been dismissed as mere verbal exercises of complacent and half-baked theorists.[1] But when they are considered in relation to their background of international and domestic politics, this impression of pretentious irrelevancy is effaced and they emerge in their true significance—as the desperate gropings of a people at war with a mighty Empire and torn by internal dissension, after a form of government which would have sufficient strength to win independence for the nation, with ample safeguards for the freedom of the individual citizen. In short, the dual conception of liberty—as freedom from alien rule and from domestic autocracy—which runs through the history of modern Greece originated with the Revolution; and the conditions that shaped the course of the struggle for independent statehood

---

[1] "The Greeks at Epidaurus did much to deceive Europe but little to organize Greece."—G. Finlay, *History of the Greek Revolution*, I, 299.

affected almost equally, though not as obviously, the quest for free government.

These conditions derived in the first place from the international situation. Being engaged in an unequal struggle against the still powerful Ottoman Empire and therefore dependent upon the good will of the neutral nations, insurgent Greece was much more imperatively committed to "a decent respect to the opinions of mankind" than were the American colonies. Moreover, under the impact of the French Revolution and Napoleon the tolerant temper of the late eighteenth century had yielded to a spirit of grim partisanship, the line of cleavage between revolution and reaction had been sharpened, and both governments and peoples had become much more keenly aware of the international implications of revolutionary movements than they were when the French monarchy and nobility blithely espoused the cause of King George III's rebellious subjects. Six years after Waterloo the attitude of world opinion on the Greek Insurrection was no more exclusively determined by its intrinsic merits than were the post-Versailles emotional alignments with respect to such movements of protest against the *status quo* as Turkish and Indian nationalism and the Russian Revolution. Because the uprising of the Greeks synchronized with the most rigorous phase of the post-Napoleonic system of peace by repression, it assumed a symbolic significance. To those who were dissatisfied with the Vienna settlement it epitomized the counteroffensive of revolution against reaction; and, by the same token, it was viewed with alarm by the governments of the great powers. Not only to Metternich, the leader of the reactionary International, and to the impressionable Alexander, but also to the relatively isolationist Castlereagh, the Greek revolt appeared "in its organization, in its objects, in its agency, and in its external relation as in no respect distinguishable from the movements in Spain, Portugal and Italy," and hence "deeply and inevitably tainted with revolutionary danger."[2] It was

---

[2] *The Cambridge History of British Foreign Policy*, ed. by Ward and Gooch, II, 85.

therefore the task of Greek diplomacy to convert into active Philhellenism the rebellious and revisionist trends of the post-Napoleonic era and, at the same time, to avoid exacerbating the reactionary governments by a too-close identification of Greek insurgency with the cause of European revolution.

This seems to have been the guiding principle of Alexander Mavrocordatos, the most western-minded politician and the foremost diplomat of Greece until the advent of Capodistrias. As president of the first National Convention he was the chief artisan of a republican and democratic constitution, the expression of the general will of the sovereign Greek people. But he was also the author of a proclamation intended for foreign consumption, which sought to justify the Insurrection as a defense of natural rights and, at the same time, emphatically dissociated it from "demagogic and revolutionary principles," and stressed its "national" character and aims.[3] The same anxiety to avoid the compromising appearance of affinity to Jacobinism—reinforced by his aversion to secret societies and his antipathy to Demetrios Ypsilantis—actuated his implacable hostility to *Hetairia Philike,* whose political eclipse was consummated in the course of the same convention largely through Mavrocordatos's efforts.[4] And even after the menace of the formation of a united reactionary front against the Insurrection had been averted, he was at pains to explain to Canning, Castlereagh's reputedly more liberal successor, that the form of government adopted by insurgent Greece was not inspired by Carbonari ideas, but was determined by the fact that the condition of equality in which the Greeks found themselves after the expulsion of their Turkish masters lent itself most readily to republican institutions.[5]

---

[3] Mamoukas, *Documents Relating to the Greek Renaissance,* II, 43. For the Proclamation of the Third National Convention see *ibid.,* VIII, 62; also Great Britain, Foreign Office, *British and Foreign State Papers* (hereafter cited as B.F.S.P.), XIII, 1062.

[4] Mavrocordatos's letter to Ypsilantis, quoted by Kordatos, *Political History of Modern Greece,* p. 270, and the Memorandum of the Metropolitan Ignatious, *ibid.,* p. 275.

[5] Mavrocordatos's letter to George Canning, Aug. 20, 1825, Dragoumes, *Historical Reminiscences,* I, 276.

This lively sense of what was diplomatically expedient in the international ambiance of the times was reflected even more strikingly in the course pursued by the Revolution on the question of the monarchy. Contrary to the assertions of rival controversialists, neither royalism nor republicanism was part of the political consciousness of the Greek people during the Insurrection.[6] The armed masses who made it, so far as they were articulate, did not formulate anything more precise than a demand for a "system" which would provide the nation with unified political and military leadership and at the same time curb the power of the sectional oligarchies.[7] The conviction that the monarchy, embodied in a foreign dynasty, was the best means of achieving national unity grew *pari passu* with the attrition and deterioration of native leadership;[8] but it was only after the interregnum of Capodistrias, the outstanding Greek of the Dispersion, ended in tragic failure that the monarchical solution proposed by the protecting powers was hopefully accepted as the only way out of anarchy. On the other hand, the usefulness of the monarchy as an instrument of diplomacy was discerned from the very beginning of the Insurrection. For it was realized that the importation of a king with the indispensable consent of the European Concert would entail the international recognition of the independence of Greece, efface the possibly embarrassing memory of the revolutionary origins of the new state, and secure for it the most favorable territorial settlement through the identification of the dynastic with the national interest.

It was this anticipation of changes dictated by the paramount exigencies of foreign policy that prompted the first National Convention to frame only a "provisional" constitution and shaped Mavrocordatos's subsequent policy. Recognizing that

[6] The ablest royalist interpretation of the Revolution is advanced by T. Pipinelis, *Political History of the Greek Revolution*. For the thesis that the Revolution was republican see J. Aravantinos, *Constitutional Law of Greece*.

[7] They were quite ready to accept such a system from a "master," i.e., a leader of the entire nation. Hence their support of Ypsilantis and later of Capodistrias, both of whom were hostile to the local oligarchies. See Kordatos, *op. cit.*, and Karl Mendelssohn-Bartholdy, *Geschichte Griechenlands*, Vol. I.

[8] Pipinelis, *op. cit.*, pp. 182, 183.

under the circumstances attending the birth of the Greek state, the question whether it would be a republic or a monarchy was primarily an international issue, he sought to extract from the manner of its settlement the maximum benefit for the national cause. Rebuffed by the European Concert while it preserved an unbroken reactionary front, he was quick to take advantage of the rift caused by Canning's advent, and during the crisis of the Egyptian invasion he made a strenuous effort to commit Great Britain to a thoroughgoing espousal of the Greek cause by thrusting upon her the role of supreme arbiter on the question of the form of government and by identifying her more closely than any of the other powers with the selection of the future dynasty of Greece. With characteristic realism he pleaded with the British Foreign Secretary for the creation of a viable state, not as a requirement of abstract justice, but as a European necessity and, more particularly, a British interest; and he affirmed the Greek people's readiness to make such changes in their governmental system as would be needed to allay the fears of the European chancelleries in exchange for the two prerequisites of viability: integral independence (as against the Russian scheme, that is, three principalities under Ottoman suzerainty), and a constitutional regime of "wise liberty."[9] Playing upon Canning's aversion to Metternich's policies and his profound distrust of Russia, he expressed the fear that, deprived of British guidance, Greece would run the risk of having foisted upon her a ruler "secretly chosen by the Holy Alliance, whom it would be impossible to reject." And since a native dynasty was not a practicable alternative, he strongly urged the British Government either to bring forward its own candidate, or to make the continuance of the existing republican regime possible by extending to it the necessary moral and material support.[10]

[9] Letter to Canning, Aug. 20, 1825, Dragoumes, *op. cit.*, p. 278. For Alexander's circular of Jan. 12, 1824, see *The Cambridge History of British Foreign Policy*, II, 87.

[10] Letter to Speliades Spaniolakis, *Reminiscences of the Greek Revolution*, II, 348–49, cited by Kordatos, *op. cit.*, p. 339. See also Tricoupis, *History of the Greek Revolution*, III, 198, and H. Temperley, *The Foreign Policy of*

Yet for all this resolute courting of British tutelage, Mavrocordatos deprecated what seemed at the time its logical culmination—the so-called "Act of Submission," by which a representative group of leaders, speaking for the Greek people, placed "the sacred deposit of its liberty, its national independence, and its political existence under the absolute protection of Great Britain."[11] As an intelligent diplomat he could foresee Canning's rejection of a course which would antagonize the other powers and disrupt what was left of the European Concert.[12] But while he deplored the diplomatic ineptness of the move, he shared the faith that inspired it. He was convinced with the majority of the Greek people that both their independence and their liberty were safer in England's keeping than they would be in the hands of any other power; that just as England could be trusted to save them from the menace of dismemberment inherent in the Russian plan, she could be equally relied upon, because of her long adherence to constitutionalism, to oppose the saddling of the new state with an absolutist system of government.[13] For whether the Greeks wanted the monarchy as the best guarantee of internal unity and stability or regarded it as a necessary concession to the anti-revolutionary and anti-republican bias of the European governments, they were agreed that it should be constitutional, that is, that its authority should be limited, not by its own will, but through the exercise of the power of the sovereign nation.

Canning, p. 341. The choice of Prince Leopold was regarded by the Greeks as "the accomplishment of the wishes expressed by themselves through the Deputation which they sent to England at an early period of their Revolution." Letter of E. J. Dawkins, Minister at Athens, to Lord Aberdeen, April 20, 1830, Inclosure in Letter of Aberdeen to Leopold, May 18, 1830, Doc. No. 41, B.F.S.P., XVII, 500.

[11] For the English text of the Act of Submission, June, 1825, see *ibid.*, XII, 904-6.

[12] Temperley, *op. cit.*, pp. 341-42; see also C. W. Crawley, *The Question of Greek Independence*, pp. 45-47.

[13] See the significant allusion of the Act of Submission to England's free institutions. In presenting the Act of Submission to Canning, the Greek Commissioners (Spaniolakis, Orlando, Louriottes) explained that "it was an act of faith in England rather than as Metternich described it, a 'renunciation of their political independence': at least they had not signed an Act of Submission to the Sultan." Crawley, *op. cit.*, p. 47.

This condition was first formulated in the provisional Constitution of eastern continental Greece, the only constitutional document of the pre-Capodistrian era which explicitly envisaged a monarchical form of government;[14] during the same period it was stressed whenever the monarchical solution was broached;[15] and it was reiterated during the Capodistrian regime, when the fourth National Convention warned both the aspirants to the Greek throne and the European powers that the definitive constitution of Greece must be founded upon the principles laid down by the assemblies of the Revolution.[16] Nor was this insistence merely a matter of decrees and formulas. That constitutional government had a meaning for the common people was revealed to President Capodistrias when a Peloponnesian peasant defined the constitution as "an agreement which prescribes our duties to you and your duties to us."[17] And that absolutism would be uncongenial to the Greeks was recognized even by the ambassadors of the protecting powers, who were sent to Greece in the autumn of 1828 in order to devise a common policy for the execution of the London Treaty of July 6, 1827.[18] The diplomatic representatives of Tory England, Czarist Russia, and Bourbon France could not, of course, endorse the Greek people's revolutionary claim to the constituent power. But they admitted that it would be "unfair and dangerous" to depart from the representative system to which the country had become accustomed under Ottoman rule and which had dominated the successive attempts to organize the state since the outbreak of the revolt. They therefore urged that the hereditary

---

[14] This sectional constitution describes the national Parliament as the *locum tenens* of the future king of Greece, whom the nation will accept from Europe provided he submits to the national laws. For the treaty see Mamoukas, *op. cit.*, I, 319.

[15] A. Londos to his constituency; P. Notaras to Londos, cited by Pipinelis, *op. cit.*, p. 183.

[16] Resolution of July 22 (August 3), 1829, Mamoukas, *op. cit.*, II, 147.

[17] Mendelssohn-Bartholdy, *op. cit.*, II, 71. Also Dragoumes, *op. cit.*, Vol. I.

[18] By the London Treaty of July 6, 1827, Great Britain, France, and Russia offered their mediation to the belligerents on the basis of the recognition of Greece as a tributary state under the sovereignty of the Sultan. For the text of the treaty see B.F.S.P., XIV, 632 ff.

monarchy, which they recommended as the most desirable regime for Greece, should be tempered by "the representative principle."[19]

II

This predilection for constitutional and representative government cannot be satisfactorily explained without reference to the internal conditions of insurgent Greece. For though primarily—and more obviously—a nationalist movement, it had two aspects. It was an effort to shake off alien rule and, concurrently, a struggle for power destined to determine the character of the nascent state. This conflict of sectional loyalties, class interests, and fierce personal antagonisms became increasingly confused as it gained in acerbity; but at the outbreak of the Insurrection it presented a fairly intelligible pattern.

Its initial phase was the clash between *Hetairia Philike,* representing in the main the *bourgeoisie* and intelligentsia of the Dispersion, and the indigenous owning and ruling classes. The secret society which inherited the tradition of Rhigas and propagated with greater conspiratorial ingenuity and success his gospel of immediate action had been too intent upon the immediate task of launching the Insurrection to formulate either long-range military plans or a program of political reconstruction. Its grandiose dream of a resuscitated Byzantine Empire through a Pan-Balkan uprising under Greek auspices came to naught with the defeat of Alexander Ypsilantis, because it was based on two false assumptions: the unwarranted reliance on the assistance of Russia, and the equally groundless expectation that the Rumanian peasantry would flock to the banner of a leader whose nationality, class, and name they associated with alien, that is, Phanariot, oppression. But while the agitation of *Philike* found a more propitious soil in Greece proper, it was handicapped by the vagueness of the plans and promises of its agents and by the resistance of those who were the logical leaders of the prospective revolt. With a vested interest in the exist-

[19] Protocol, London, July 1, 1830, Doc. No. 33, *ibid.,* XVIII, 605.

ing order and mindful of their personal accountability to the Ottoman Government for the loyalty of its Greek subjects, the indigenous ruling classes—Peloponnesian landowners, Hydriot shipowners and merchants, and higher clergy—hesitated to plunge into insurgency at the behest of rootless idealists and, at worst, irresponsible adventurers. Moreover, having experienced as late as 1770 the tragic consequences of trustful reliance on Russia, they were unimpressed by the studiously vague promises of support from the same quarter. Nor was the insistence of the agents of *Philike* upon the necessity of surrendering all power into the hands of a mysterious "Supreme Authority" calculated to reassure those who had to all intents and purposes governed Greece under Ottoman rule. And their uneasiness on this score was intensified by the eager response of two other elements of the population to the propaganda of immediate action: the chieftains of the armed irregulars and the common people, to whom insurrection held out the prospect not only of national independence but also of economic and social betterment. But those considerations of self-interest were outweighed by the solidarity born of religious affinity and the essential equality in subjection which was the lot of all the Greeks in relation to their Ottoman masters. Hence the leading Peloponnesian notables compromised themselves irretrievably by becoming initiated into *Philike*. But, distrustful of the most reckless of its agitators and filled with misgivings, they decided as late as February 8, 1821, that "even if the expected plenipotentiary of the Supreme Authority arrived, the Peloponnesus would not move before the other parts of Greece."[20] This reluctance was even more pronounced in the case of the upper class of the Aegean Islands and, especially, the masterful Hydriot shipowners, who, though destined to become the financial and maritime bulwark of the Revolution, were driven by popular pressure into joining it one month after its outbreak on the mainland. It would, therefore, be reasonable to conclude

[20] Tricoupis, *op. cit.*, I, 25, and A. Dascalakis, *Causes and Factors of the Greek Revolution of 1821*, p. 80.

that the Insurrection was prepared and instigated in the main by the Greeks of the Dispersion and was begun by the spontaneous and isolated action of local military chieftains supported by the common people—the peasants of the Peloponnesus, the shepherds and graziers of continental Greece, the sailors of the islands and the lower clergy. The upper clergy and the ruling oligarchy, confronted with the dilemma of answering with life and property for the insurgency of their humbler co-religionists[21] or of blocking the path of national liberation, were virtually compelled to assume the leadership of the revolt. But they did so with the perfectly understandable expectation that national independence, by removing the control of the Ottoman Government, would consolidate rather than impair their traditional primacy.

Thus, shortly after the initial outbreaks in Achaia and Maina insurgent Greece had achieved an essential unity of purpose. The acts of insurgency against the Empire were irrevocable, and there was no alternative to the prosecution of the struggle for any class or section of the nation. The next urgent task was to implement this spiritual unity with the requisite political institutions and military instruments; and to this task Demetrios Ypsilantis addressed himself, as soon as he arrived in Greece as the "plenipotentiary" of his brother Alexander and hence the most proximate incarnation of the more or less mythical "Supreme Authority" preached by *Philike*. He proposed to organize Greece, beginning with the Peloponnesus, along unitary lines by (*a*) creating a national Parliament vested with both legislative and executive powers, (*b*) making himself its President, and, (*c*) in that capacity, both the chief executive of the nation and the commander in chief of its armed forces, and (*d*) setting up in every one of the existing administrative areas a committee of elected officials (*ephors*) to act both as local administrators and as the agents of the central

---

[21] The invitation of the Peloponnesian notables to Tripoli early in March to "confer" with the Governor left no doubt in their minds that they were to be held as hostages.

government.[22] Pending the creation of a national parliament, he recognized the sectional council of notables which called itself the Peloponnesian Senate, but he rejected its interference in the conduct of military operations except those involving the dispatch of Peloponnesian troops beyond the Peloponnesus, which he agreed to undertake only with the Senate's consent.[23]

This plan, which aimed to lodge supreme power in one man and to provide him, by popular election, with the necessary instruments of centralized control was naturally unpalatable to the ruling oligarchy. Yet their counter proposals were remarkably conciliatory. They rejected the abolition of the Peloponnesian Senate; but they offered Ypsilantis its presidency, with concurrent powers[24] and the right to break a tie with his vote. And on the question of the high command they yielded to the extent of making him the chairman (with a casting vote) of a war-council of three appointed by the Senate.[25]

Had Ypsilantis been an experienced politician, he would have either immediately agreed to this compromise or mobilized sufficient mass support to coerce his opponents into acceptance of his terms. For the common people, instructed by the agents of *Philike*, were eager to follow his leadership, resented the opposition of the Peloponnesian oligarchy, and on at least one occasion were prevented from drastic resort to direct action only by the timely intervention of Colocotronis, who dispersed an armed mob about to attack the notables with the warning that internecine strife would create the impression in Europe that the Greeks were "Carbonari and agents of disorder and lawlessness."[26] But while Ypsilantis was probably the most disinterested leader of the Revolution and was to prove himself resourceful and fearless on the battlefield, he was neither a politician nor a tribune of the people. His claim to supreme power had been weakened by his brother's defeat in Wallachia and

---

[22] Mamoukas, *op. cit.*, I, 9.
[23] *Ibid.*, p. 17.
[24] "Neither the Prince shall undertake anything without the Senate's consent, nor the Senate without the consent of the Prince." *Ibid.*, p. 13.
[25] *Ibid.*, p. 16.   [26] See Mendelssohn-Bartholdy, *op. cit.*, I, 350–52.

could only be revalidated with the consent of the Greek people. Had he placed himself at the head of a popular movement in order to wrest this consent from a recalcitrant and powerful minority, he would have disrupted the unity of the nation and converted what he conceived to be a war of national liberation into a domestic class-struggle. This course, which was urged upon him by his more radical lieutenants and agents of *Philike,* he refused to follow. He retained the nominal leadership of the Revolution until the meeting of the first National Convention; but his failure to strike at the decisive moment condemned him to gradual political eclipse, which was accelerated by the impairment of the prestige of *Philike* and the rapid shifts in the balance of power among the contending forces. Though he was eventually elected to the presidency of the Peloponnesian Senate, the sectional constitution framed by that body conceded to him much less than the compromise originally proposed by the notables. The primacy of the national Parliament was recognized in theory; but the extensive powers retained by the Senate presaged a regime of "dual sovereignty," which strengthened Peloponnesian particularism and sowed the seeds of civil war.[27]

III

That unity could not be achieved by the concentration of power in the hands of a rank outsider and the relegation of the indigenous leaders to a subordinate position was clearly discerned by Ypsilantis's fellow-Phanariot and bitter rival, Alexander Mavrocordatos. The foremost of the intellectuals of the Dispersion, he had no class attachments in Greece and hence no vested interest in the preservation of the existing order. His preference for a unitary system was therefore dictated both by the ambition to play a prominent part in the revolution and by the conviction that unity was a political and military necessity. But being as good a politician as Ypsilantis was a soldier, he recognized the futility of attempting to browbeat the ruling

[27] Constitution of the Peloponnesian Senate signed Dec. 27, 1821 (Jan. 9, 1832). Mamoukas, *op. cit.,* I, 107.

oligarchy into abdication by a mere flourish of credentials. On the other hand, he perceived that while refusing to surrender to a dictator, the Peloponnesian notables might not be averse to a unitary state in which, given the existing balance of forces, they could reasonably expect to retain a controlling influence; and he realized that the only effective retort to this Peloponnesian claim to primacy was the mobilization of the political and military resources of the other sections of Greece.

With this end in view he secured Ypsilantis's permission to organize continental Greece, thus providing himself with a territorial base for his prospective political career. And he further strengthened his position by assiduously cultivating the shipowning and mercantile plutocracy of the Aegean Islands, who were the natural opponents both of the landowning Peloponnesian oligarchy and of the popular elements that constituted the potential following of Ypsilantis and *Philike*. These politic moves and his incontestable intellectual distinction secured for him a dominant position in the first National Convention which, under his presidency, attempted to organize a "political system," that is, to draw up a constitution, for the whole of insurgent Greece.[28]

This system was, in the last analysis, a compromise between the ideal of national unity and the stubborn realities that blocked its translation into institutions. Even the most sectionally-minded oligarchs agreed with the intellectuals that only a central government, acting as the instrument of a sovereign national state, could prosecute the war successfully and conduct an effective foreign policy. But the compulsive power of this conviction was reduced by contact with such facts as sectional patriotism, the temper of the ruling classes, the vague but potentially explosive aspirations of the common people, and the inveterate insubordination of the local war lords. The result of this conflict of interests and confusion of motives was a constitution which postulated a unitary state and a central

[28] Letter of the Hydriots to the Peloponnesian Senate urging immediate convocation of a National Convention, quoted by Kordatos, *op. cit.*, p. 274.

government but at the same time was inspired throughout by fear of what must have seemed to its framers the most obvious concomitant of political unity—the concentration of power in any individual, group, or geographical section. Though the provisions and the terminology of the constitution were borrowed from the constitutional literature of the French Revolution, its substance was clearly intended to reduce to a minimum the sacrifices of those already in power. Hence principles and devices such as the separation of powers, a crude system of checks and balances, a collegiate executive, a preponderant legislature, and annual appeals to the electorate were resorted to because they all made for a diffusion of power and in the last analysis nullified the theoretical acceptance of the unitary principle by impeding the exercise of unitary control.

These generalizations are borne out by an examination of the main provisions of the constitution. It set up a unicameral legislature, elected annually, which checked the executive at every step without, however, being exposed to the retaliation of dissolution. The legislature was empowered to initiate legislation, vote the budget, and confirm all military appointments. Its consent was necessary for the declaration of war, the conclusion of peace or of any other treaty, the contracting of a loan, and the mortgaging or expropriation of "national property."[29] It could initiate impeachment proceedings and by a vote of four-fifths of its members could depose and hand over to the courts for trial any member of the executive accused of high treason or other "political crimes."

As regards the executive, the constitution[30] provided for a committee of five elected annually outside the membership of the legislature by an *ad hoc* assembly. It performed its administrative functions through a ministry of eight, headed by the Secretary of State. It shared the legislative initiative, participated through the appropriate ministers in the legislative process,

[29] The Turkish landed and other property, public and private, which was transferred to the nation as a result of the overthrow of Turkish rule.
[30] The text of the constitution is in Mamoukas, *op. cit.*, II, 13. See also Aravantinos, *op. cit.*, p. 156.

and was vested with the veto power. Its collegiate composition (obviously adapted from the Constitution of the Year III), in conjunction with the shortness of its term of office, was designed to raise a barrier to individual ascendancy and at the same time to make the central government representative of all the four sections of insurgent Greece.[31] But the relations of the sectional governments to the central government were not defined, though the supremacy of the latter was explicitly affirmed.[32]

The second National Convention recognized the incompatibility of the sectional governments with a unitary system and decreed their abolition.[33] At the same time, plagued by the insubordination of the military chieftains and by the demand of Colocotronis for the permanent high command of the Peloponnesian levies, it attempted to formulate with greater precision the doctrine of the supremacy of the civil government. "In accord with the example of the wise nations of the world," it laid down the principle that (a) "the command of the national land and sea forces being vested exclusively in the central government, the title of commander-in-chief either for Greece as a whole or for any of its sections is absolutely inacceptable to the Greek nation"; and (b) "such a title may be conferred by the government for a specific campaign, at the end of which the incumbent must resume his previous rank."[34] The price of this defiance of the military was another concession to sectionalism. For in order to equip the central government with sufficient authority to enforce its writ the Minister of War and the Secretary of the Navy were replaced by two committees of three, representing, respectively, the Peloponnesus, continental Greece and Maina, that is, the parts of Greece which were most active in the war on land, and the three "maritime islands" (Hydra, Spezzia, and Psara), which bore the brunt of the naval opera-

[31] The sectional distribution of the first Executive was as follows: A. Mavrocordatos, President (Western Continental Greece), A. Kanakares, Vice-President, and Papayannopoulos (Peloponnesus), J. Orlandos (Islands) and J. Logothetis (Eastern Continental Greece), Mamoukas, *op. cit.*, II, 52.
[32] Article CI, *ibid.*, pp. 13 ff.
[33] Decree of March 30 (April 12), 1823, Mamoukas, *op. cit.*, II, 98.
[34] Decree of March 29 (April 11), 1823, *ibid.*, p. 85.

tions.[35] But while these administrative changes might have strengthened the central government, two constitutional amendments enacted by the Convention tended to reduce it to impotence. The first of these curtailed the legislative initiative of the executive and reduced its power to stop legislation to a suspensive veto;[36] and the second—deliberately patterned after the analogous powers of the American Senate—conferred upon the legislature concurrent powers in the appointment of prefects, a concession which was extended in practice to every rank of government officials.[37]

The inevitable result of this confusion of powers was an incessant conflict between the two bodies, which, aggravated by sectional antagonism, the insubordination of the military chieftains, and bitter personal feuds, produced a state of virtual anarchy. The civil war toward which the country had been drifting broke out in the late autumn of 1824, when Colocotronis and the Peloponnesian notables, that is, the military and the political elements of Peloponnesian particularism, united by their common grievances, openly defied the central government which was dominated by the Hydriots and Mavrocordatos. With the help of the hardy Rumeliots (the troops of continental Greece) under John Kolettes, the government won what turned out to be a Pyrrhic victory. For the defeat of the Peloponnesian forces and the imprisonment of Colocotronis, who combined military ability of high order with extraordinary capacity for popular leadership, left what was by all odds the most important province of insurgent Greece defenseless against the invasion of Ibrahim's modernized armies. The ensuing disasters had far-reaching political repercussions. The resignation of the executive headed by the Hydriot George Coundouriotis terminated the ascendancy of what might be called the constitutionalist party of Mavrocordatos and the shipowners of Hydra and Spezzia, who, intermittently supported by the democratic ele-

[35] *Ibid.*
[36] Article XVII of the revised Constitution.
[37] Decree of April 13, 1823, Mamoukas, *op. cit.,* III, 8, and Dragoumes, *op. cit.,* I, 31.

ments of continental Greece, had attempted to assert the supremacy of a central government representing the entire nation.[38]

The failure of this attempt, synchronizing as it did with the most disastrous phase of the war, marked the nadir of the Revolution. When the third National Convention met in the midst of the Egyptian invasion and on the eve of the fall of Messolonghi, it recognized the futility of protracted constitution-mongering at a time when the very existence of the nation was in doubt. With a view to "concentrating the executive power" in order to meet the desperate military situation "with efficiency and dispatch,"[39] it set up an emergency government consisting of two commissions, the first of which was entrusted with internal administration and national defense and the second with the conduct of foreign relations. A series of carefully drafted decrees (which showed greater familiarity with procedure and a keener sense of constitutional propriety than did previous similar documents) defined the functions of these bodies, laid down the principle that they derived their mandate from and were accountable to the Convention, directed the Commission on Foreign Policy to invoke British mediation with a view to terminating hostilities, and gave it precise instructions for its guidance in negotiating peace.[40]

This emergency regime, which was dominated by the Peloponnesian notables under Andrew Zaimis, proved unequal to the herculean task of unifying the country and resisting the invader. Though the Insurrection was revived in continental Greece by the brilliant campaign of Karaïskakis, it was reduced to a sporadic and intermittent flicker in the Peloponnesus, where rival factions and rump assemblies disputed from sheer force of habit for the control of a country that had been almost completely overrun by the Egyptian steam roller. When the third National Convention finally reassembled in Troezene, the conviction that polyarchy spelled anarchy and impotence had been borne

[38] Pipinelis, *op. cit.*, pp. 171, 172, 173.
[39] Preamble to the Decree of April 12, 1826, Mamoukas, *op. cit.*, IV, 103.
[40] *Ibid.*, IV, 79, 80, 90–110, and V, 1–16.

in upon the most recalcitrant.[41] A new humility, born of adversity, made submission to unitary control all the easier because, owing to the attrition of native leadership, the supreme power could no longer be claimed by any of the prominent political or military figures of the Revolution. This contrite spirit was reflected in the acceptance of Colocotronis's proposal to surrender the high command of the army and the navy to rank outsiders (the well-meaning but inadequate Church and the self-seeking adventurer Cochrane) and to elect the foremost Greek of the Dispersion to the presidency.[42]

The constitution drafted by the Convention after the election of Capodistrias was designed to avert whatever dangers might inhere in a single executive by a precise delimitation of its powers. The president, elected for a term of seven years, was made "inviolable," that is, his political responsibility devolved upon the ministers who composed his cabinet and whose constitutional status was defined in (*a*) the provision requiring the countersignature of a minister to all state documents, and (*b*) the liability of ministers to impeachment by the legislature.[43] Denied access to the legislature except at the opening and at the closing sitting of every session, the president was represented in that body by the ministers, who, though not eligible to it, were admitted to all its sittings, introduced the budget and other bills of executive origin and answered questions and interpellations concerning the government's policies.[44]

The legislature was made completely independent of the executive. It was elected for a term of three years, and one-third of its membership was replenished annually. It convened on the first Monday of October for its regular session of "four to five" months and was not subject to dissolution by the president, who could, however, prolong its regular session or convoke

[41] See, for instance, the Memorandum addressed to the Convention by Colocotronis, *ibid.*, VII, 103.
[42] Proceedings of the Third National Convention, March 30 (April 12), 1827, *ibid.*, pp. 94–103.
[43] Articles CVI, CXXVII, CXXX, CXXXIII; for text of the Constitution of Troezene, May, 1827, see *ibid.*, IX, 128 ff., and B.F.S.P., XV, 1069 ff.
[44] Articles LXXVII, CXVIII, CXXVIII, CXXIX, *loc. cit.*

it to a special session "depending on the needs of the state."[45] He shared the legislative initiative and exercised it through his ministers. But while he could not introduce government bills after a third rejection by the legislature, he could not withhold his assent from a measure initiated by the legislature if it was passed for a third time over his veto.[46]

It is evident from this summary analysis that the Constitution of 1827, apart from the innovation in the matter of the presidency, reflected the same aversion to a strong executive and preference for a preponderant legislature that characterized its predecessor; and it gave much more precise expression to this essentially democratic temper by a stricter application of the principle of the separation of powers. At the same time it marked a distinct advance in (*a*) its explicit affirmation of the principle of popular sovereignty,[47] (*b*) its recognition of the distinction between the legislative and the constituent process,[48] and (*c*) its keener awareness of and elaborate provision for civil liberty. The Bill of Rights which was attached to it guaranteed equality before the law, equal eligibility to public office, security of life, liberty, and property, freedom of speech and of the press; it outlawed slavery, banned titles of nobility, excluded the clergy from public office, insured freedom of worship for all religions, and, except for the provisions which made the Eastern Orthodox Church the religion of the state and adherence to Christianity prerequisite to citizenship, followed the most advanced declaration of the French Revolution.[49] Designed, in the words of its framers, to "establish and guarantee the rights" and to "exercise the sovereignty" of the Greek people,[50] the constitution was stillborn precisely because it was considered too liberal and democratic to be an effective instrument

---

[45] Articles LVII, LVIX, LX, CXIV, *loc. cit.*
[46] Articles LXXIII and LXV, *loc. cit.*
[47] Article V, *loc. cit.*
[48] Article LXCIV, *loc. cit.*
[49] Articles V and XXVIII, *loc. cit.*
[50] Proclamation of the Third National Convention accompanying the Promulgation of the Constitution, Mamoukas, *op. cit.*, IX, 58. See also B.F.S.P., XV, 1067 ff.

of crisis government. But its Bill of Rights, which embodied the ideal of the rule of law and respect for the rights of the citizen, has survived as the strongest weapon of liberty against autocracy through the many political changes of more than one hundred years of Greek history.

IV

While the concepts and terminology of the pre-Capodistrian constitutions were borrowed from Revolutionary France, the principles of representation and the methods of election followed during the same period did not depart materially from indigenous custom. The first National Convention was not elected by direct popular vote. It was composed of delegates of the Aegean Islands and the three sectional assemblies (the Peloponnesus, Eastern Continental Greece, and Western Continental Greece); and these assemblies in turn had been elected by the customary methods prevalent in each section under the Ottoman system of communal autonomy.[51] Hence the membership of the Convention consisted of the lay and clerical leaders of the various localities before the Insurrection; and except for the relative preponderance of a new element, the intellectuals of the Dispersion who had flocked to Greece after the outbreak of the revolt, it could be said to be as representative of the nation as if it had been elected directly and by means of a more uniformly democratic franchise. This was probably less true of the legislature of thirty-three members, under the presidency of Ypsilantis, which the Convention set up without recourse to a national election in order to expedite the organization of the government.[52]

The second National Convention, on the other hand, seems to have seated many would-be delegates without insisting on the authenticity of their credentials;[53] and it admitted to membership not only government appointees but also any members of

---

[51] See chap. i, *supra*, pp. 28–29; Mamoukas, *op. cit.*, I, 85–123, and Dragoumes, *op. cit.*, I, 28. For Capodistrias's reply to the Conference of Ambassadors see Mamoukas, *op. cit.*, II, 329.
[52] *Ibid.*, pp. 53–56.
[53] Dragoumes, *op. cit.*, p. 35.

the incumbent executive and legislature "who desired to contribute to its deliberations and sign its decrees."[54] The result was a fluctuating membership which reached the staggering total of two hundred and sixty-five signatories of the revised constitution, as against fifty-nine who had signed the original promulgated by the first Convention.[55] The anti-oligarchic and egalitarian temper of this motley assembly was reflected in a constitutional amendment apparently intended to safeguard the "national estates" against wholesale purchase by the big landowners,[56] and in an additional "interpretative decree," which inferentially placed an embargo on the sale of land by enumerating the various items of national property that could be acquired by individuals.[57]

The "Provisional Electoral Law," of November 9 (22), 1822, "enacted by the legislature and ratified by the executive," was the first attempt to establish a uniform franchise. It distributed the seats in the national legislature on the basis of one member for every twenty-five thousand of the population, but allotted seven members to the "maritime islands" (three to Hydra and two each to Spezzia and Psara) in recognition of their importance as the naval strongholds of the nation. It provided for indirect election of members of the legislature—by delegates of the communes who composed the electoral college of each district (*eparchoi*). It conferred eligibility to the legislature upon Greek citizens twenty-five years of age who were either natives of the district or residents for five years and owners of real property.[58] Both in its adherence to the principle of indirect election and in its vagueness with regard to the qualifications of the voters the law was merely a rather crude codification of the prevailing electoral practice. Its only important innovation, the article which provided for the election of the five members

---

[54] Mamoukas, *op. cit.*, p. 91.
[55] *Ibid.*, p. 148, and Dragoumes, *op. cit.*, p. 36.
[56] Article XXXV of the revised constitution, Mamoukas, *op. cit.*, p. 127.
[57] These items were houses and vacant lots, stores, inns, public baths, mosques, and adjoining schoolhouses (*medressé*), bakeries, and oil presses. Decree of April 14, 1823.
[58] Articles II, III, IV, and V, *ibid.*, III, 69.

CONSTITUTIONS OF THE REVOLUTION

of the executive by the legislature, betrayed the intellectual confusion of its authors—whether viewed as a violation of the constitution or as an unconscious usurpation of the constituent power.[59]

The same conservatism characterized the administrative system of the Revolution. The fundamental principle of municipal and provincial autonomy under Ottoman rule had been the devolution of local administration upon locally elected officials who were ultimately accountable to the central government. This relationship was maintained during the Insurrection with the basic difference that the state was no longer an alien despotism but was a more or less democratic republic deriving its powers from the sovereign Greek people. The second National Convention promulgated an amended "law for the organization of the provinces of Greece," which had been enacted by the first legislature. It divided the country into communes, townships, and eparchies. It entrusted the administration of the two smaller divisions to elected elders and of the eparchies to five officials, two of whom, the controller of revenues and the controller of expenditures, were elected, and the other three, the prefect (*eparch*), the secretary-general, and the chief constable, were appointed by the central government.[60] It provided that the eparch could not be a native of his eparchy —a prohibition apparently intended to prevent the local oligarchies from further entrenching themselves and to strengthen the authority of the central government over its agents of provincial administration. It decreed that each eparchy should provide one-third of its constabulary, conferred extensive powers on the elders of the communes and townships, but placed them under the jurisdiction of the eparch, whom in turn, along with both the appointed and the elected officials of the eparchy, it made responsible to the Minister of the Interior representing

[59] The law was apparently the work of Theodore Negris, a rather uncritical theorist, the author of the Provisional Constitution of Western Continental Greece. The decree was signed by Negris, as Secretary of State, and in the absence of Mavrocordatos, the President of the Executive, by A. Kanakares, the Vice-President.

[60] No. 12 of the Code of Laws, Mamoukas, *op. cit.*, III, 60.

the central government. This combination of local initiative and administrative decentralization with ultimate responsibility to the center and centralized control was an adaptation of the system of communal autonomy to the new conditions created by the abolition of Ottoman rule. The revision effected by the third National Convention, except for the superimposition of larger administrative units, to which were given the Byzantine name Themes, did not depart materially from these principles.[61] And though the measure finally voted by the *Panhellenion,* the first legislature of the Capodistrian regime, expanded the jurisdiction of the central government, it was not as destructive of local autonomy as it has been represented by the President's critics.[62]

Even if the leaders of insurgent Greece had been masters of statecraft, they would probably have proved unequal to the task of creating a state in the midst of a desperate struggle to wrest recognition of the nation's right to independent statehood. Had they been permitted to indulge in calm reflection and to take "the long view," they might have concluded that the particularism of the various sections, which was the product both of the geography and of the history of Greece, was the ideal prerequisite to a federal form of government, and that a federal system, evolved gradually and grounded in the sectional loyalties and the institutions of local self-government inherited from the past, would make ultimately for greater national unity. On the other hand, the immediate organization of the nation along unitary lines was dictated by the compelling exigencies of war and diplomacy; it could be justified by the example of Revolutionary France and supported by the consensus of contemporary opinion, which considered federalism as quite unsuited to small countries. The gaping discrepancies between the actualities of insurgent Greece and the constitutions and the laws designed to create a unitary state, should not completely obscure

[61] Decree of May 1, 1827, *ibid.,* IX, 121.
[62] Decree No. 1747, *ibid.,* II, 395; Capodistrias's instructions, *ibid.,* p. 396. Dragoumes, *op. cit.,* I, 107, is to be contrasted with Argyropoulos, *op. cit.* See chap. iii, *infra.*

the ideological significance and the educative influence of these documents. For though essentially derivative, loosely drawn, and often contradictory, they translated into constitutional and legal concepts the democratic, liberal, and egalitarian temper of the Greek people. It is because they were, despite the imitativeness of their form, essentially indigenous in substance, that they laid the ground work of a liberal and constitutionalist tradition which, after making itself immediately felt against President Capodistrias, was to endure and grow to the present day.

Chapter Three

THE CAPODISTRIAN DICTATORSHIP

I

BETWEEN the date of the election of Capodistrias and his arrival in Greece the Insurrection had been salvaged by two decisive events. The London Treaty of July 6, 1827, committed Great Britain, France, and Russia to mediation on the basis of a settlement favorable to Greece; while the victory of the combined British, French, and Russian fleets at Navarino reinforced this commitment and marked the beginning of the end of the Egyptian invasion. Nevertheless, President Capodistrias was still faced with a formidable task—diplomatic, political, and administrative. The basic constitutional problem of his administration arose from the fact that the active leadership which the nature of his task called for and which he was eager to exercise was quite incompatible with the passive role assigned to the president by the Constitution of Troezene. In the conflict precipitated by this incompatibility Capodistrias ranged himself against liberalism and constitutionalism as currently understood in the nineteenth century; and in his foreign policy he relied more on autocratic Russia than on Tory England or legitimist France. That these circumstances contributed materially to the harsh judgment passed upon him by liberal and Russophobe historians is a reasonable assumption. Their disparaging estimate has been summed up in characterizations indicative of their bias—such as the reproach that he was "born under the Venetian oligarchy and brought up in a despot's court"[1] and the charge that the policies he pursued in Greece were worthy of "a former minister of the Holy Alliance"[2] and "a Russian

[1] Mendelssohn-Bartholdy, *Geschichte Griechenlands*, II, 18–19.
[2] Georg Gottfried Gervinus, *Geschichte des neunzehnten Jahrhunderts seit den Wiener vertragen*.

pro-Consul."[3] A reappraisal of his statesmanship, however, both before and after he assumed the presidency of Greece, calls for considerable modification of this summary verdict.

To such a reappraisal three phases of Capodistrias's career before 1827 are especially relevant: (a) his political novitiate in the Ionian Islands during the turbulent first decade of the nineteenth century; (b) his mission to Switzerland as the representative of Czar Alexander; and (c) his share in shaping the foreign policy of Russia after the defeat of Napoleon. In the course of this varied activity he developed an increasingly consistent political philosophy, which decisively influenced the policies he devised for the governance of Greece.

Though an aristocrat by birth, Capodistrias did not align himself with his class in the struggle which was precipitated by the French occupation of the Ionian Islands. He made his political début in the course of the popular outbreaks against the so-called "Byzantine Constitution" of 1800, by which the aristocratic party, taking advantage of the expulsion of the French by the Russians, attempted to restore the ultra-oligarchic regime of the Venetian era.[4] As one of the imperial commissioners entrusted with the restoration of order and, immediately afterward, as Provisional Governor of Cephalonia, the most democratic of the Islands, he impressed upon the people that, while hostile to revolution inspired by the French example, he was equally opposed to the restoration of the social and political system which had been overthrown by the French occupation. He gave concrete expression to his political views when, as Secretary of State, he contributed decisively to the drafting of the Constitution of 1803, which deprived the hereditary nobility of the monopoly of power by admitting to the electoral college the propertied and educated classes, recognized Greek as the official language, and made the Eastern Orthodox Church the state religion of the Heptanesian Republic.[5] And though he

[3] Mendelssohn-Bartholdy, *loc. cit.* See also Finlay, *History of the Greek Revolution;* J. A. Gobineau, *Deux études sur la Grèce moderne; Capodistrias, le royaume des Hellènes.*
[4] Cf. p. 23, *supra.*
[5] For other provisions of the Constitution of 1803 see p. 26, *supra.*

subsequently consented to certain concessions to the conservatives calculated to placate Russia, he strenuously resisted the aristocratic party's efforts to restrict the franchise and to regain its political supremacy. Thus by the time he left the Islands (because he refused to serve under the French to whom they had been ceded by the Tilsit agreements) Capodistrias had developed a political creed from which he did not materially depart in later life. Its main articles were: hostility to revolution, Jacobinism and Bonapartism, opposition to the *ancien régime,* and the rule of the hereditary aristocracy, advocacy of the gradual and orderly political enfranchisement of the productive classes of society, beginning with the middle class, faith in the efficacy of education, and the conviction that adherence to traditional religion and the cultivation of the Greek language would contribute powerfully to the preservation of Greek nationality.

Capodistrias's mission to Switzerland was in its essentials a duplication on a larger scale of his work in the Ionian Islands. The defeat of Napoleon and the violation of Swiss neutrality by the Austro-Russian armies having brought to an end the regime established in 1803 by the Act of Mediation, the aristocratic party undertook, under the aegis of Metternich, to restore the *status quo* anterior to the French occupation and the establishment of the Helvetian Republic. But such a complete surrender to reaction was opposed by Czar Alexander, who was then passing through the liberal phase of his international Messianism, and whose Swiss policy was largely shaped by the influence of La Harpe, his former teacher and the boldest exponent of democracy and nationalism in Switzerland. It was because he was known to be equally opposed to the restoration of the *ancien régime* that Capodistrias was entrusted by the Czar (first as his semi-official diplomatic agent and later as minister plenipotentiary of Russia) with the congenial task of checkmating Metternich and the aristocratic party.[6] "I desire,"

---

[6] "Il est de Corfu; par consequent républicain. Et c'est la connaissance de ses principes qui me l'a fait choisir." Correspondance d' Alexandre et Leopold, *Imperial Russian Archeological Society,* I, 44. See also A. M. Idromenos, *J. Capodistrias.*

ran Alexander's "special instructions" to his Minister, "that the happiness of Switzerland should derive from the welfare of all classes and of all cantons. I will not allow any ancient institutions to stand in the way of these principles and of these views."[7] Capodistrias faithfully strove to carry out these instructions in the midst of an extremely fluid and complicated situation. His policy was based on the theory that "the spirit which brought about the revolution in Switzerland had made itself felt long before the outbreak of the French Revolution, and it arose from popular discontent caused by the aristocratic institutions of monopoly and subjection."[8] But while he thus disassociated the transformation effected since 1798 from the French Revolution, he accepted both the social reforms and the most fundamental of the political changes, that is, the admission to the Federation of the democratic cantons created by the Act of Mediation, as essential to the reconstruction of Switzerland. Equally hostile to the two extremes—the loose federalism of the aristocratic cantons and the Jacobin centralization of the Helvetian Republic—he advocated the formation of a closely-knit federal union comprising both the old and the new, the aristocratic and the democratic cantons, with a strong central government.[9] The Federal Pact, which emerged from deliberations of the "Long Diet,"[10] on August 16, 1819, disappointed him to the extent that it created a loose confederacy of practically sovereign cantons with a powerless central government—a return to the state of things anterior to 1798.[11] Nevertheless, at the Congress of Vienna, as the chief Russian adviser on Swiss

[7] William Martin, *La Suisse et l'Europe, 1813-1814*.

[8] Memorandum to Committee on Swiss Affairs (in Congress of Vienna), S. T. Lascaris, *Capodistrias avant la Révolution grecque, sa carrière politique jusqu'en 1822; étude d'histoire diplomatique et de droit international*, p. 71.

[9] Memorandum to the Diet on the Swiss Constitution, April 21, 1814, Lascaris, *op. cit.*, p. 50. See also von Muyden, *Histoire de la nation Suisse*, III, 168.

[10] "C'est en effet Capodistrias qui avait reçu la mission de surveiller les débats constitutionnels de la Diète, et d'aider à la confection du nouveau Pacte Fédéral, dont elle poussait péniblement le travail." Edouard L. M. Guillon, *Napoléon et la Suisse, 1803-1815*, p. 292.

[11] Gonzague de Reynold, *La Démocratie et la Suisse*, p. 221. In his farewell address to the Diet, he declared that the constitution was bad, but expressed the hope that with good faith on all sides it might work—"car ce sont les hommes plus que les constitutions qui sont l'affaire importante dans le gouvernement." Lascaris, *op. cit.*, p. 60.

affairs, he vigorously upheld the inclusiveness of the Pact, defended the integrity of the new cantons, and successfully resisted their mediatization by the aristocratic cantons in the name of the principle of legitimacy.[12]

The same moderate liberalism, compounded of equal hostility to revolution and to reaction, inspired his recommendations to the Czar with regard to the reconstruction of Europe after the fall of Napoleon. He strove, not without success, to persuade Alexander that the policy of leniency toward France should be persisted in even after the Hundred Days. With respect to the future regime of that country he was, as an enemy of Jacobinism and Bonapartism, a convinced legitimist; but at the same time, he advocated "a constitution which would establish the power of the king's government firmly on a national representative body and would identify the interests created by twenty-five years of revolution with those of the monarchy."[13] He contributed to the early readmission of France into the European Concert; but he vigorously combated the so-called "Congress System," which in final analysis placed both the custody of the international *status quo* and the governance of the lesser states of Europe in the hands of the great powers. To Metternich's consistent interventionism he opposed the view that the governments of the leading powers "should not permit themselves to decide on any affair which concerned the other states unless formally invited, and should then admit them to their deliberations."[14] At the Congress of Troppau, which brought the conflict of the two diplomats to a head, Capodistrias objected to the dispatch of Austrian troops to Naples unless they went as a "European army" and promised to establish "in agreement with the King, a form of government which would ensure to the Neapolitans the peaceful enjoyment of two-fold freedom—

---

[12] For memoranda of Nov. 12, 1814, and Jan. 16, 1815, to Committee on Swiss Affairs see Lascaris, *ibid.*, pp. 70–73.

[13] Memorandum of July 28, 1815, Lascaris, *op. cit.*, p. 77.

[14] Quoted by Lascaris, *op. cit.*, p. 99, as found in F. de Martens, *Recueil de traités et conventions conclus par la Russie*, VII, 296.

national and political."[15] In other words, he advocated intervention on behalf of liberalism and nationalism; and he envisaged the Concert of Europe, not as a consistent defender of the *status quo,* but as a mediator between monarchs and peoples, aiming to avert revolution by combating reaction, that is, by satisfying popular aspirations to political liberty and national independence. Hence, it is not to be wondered at that Metternich regarded the Czar's "more Greek than Russian minister" as an "ardent champion of doctrinaire liberalism," and singled him out as his most redoubtable opponent in the struggle for the mastery of Alexander's soul.[16] When the Austrian Chancellor confided to his *Memoirs* that his antagonist was "not a bad man" but "a complete, a thorough fool, a perfect miracle of wrongheadedness" and that he lived in "a world to which our minds are often transported by a bad nightmare,"[17] he gave vent to his exasperation at Capodistrias's tenacity and to the anxiety he felt over the influence of such a minister on the impressionable Russian emperor. "The struggle between Capodistrias and me," he wrote on another occasion with characteristic complacency, "is like the conflict between a positive and a negative force."[18] The Austrian chancellor's victory in this struggle was due precisely to the fact that Capodistrias did not possess the attributes of a "minister of the Holy Alliance." He had endeavored instead to be a good European, and it was more than a coincidence that his ascendancy synchronized with Alexander's liberal phase, while the decline of his influence

[15] Memorandum to Troppau Congress, cited by Stern, *Geschichte Europas,* II, 130.
[16] "Capodistrias, Metternich felt, stood between him and Alexander. . . . Capodistrias, who had no Austrian sympathies and who disliked Metternich even before Metternich had done him any harm, was able, ambitious, and far-seeing." Hélène du Coudray, *Metternich,* p. 194.
[17] *Memoirs of Prince Metternich,* ed. by Prince Richard Metternich; tr. by Mrs. Alexander Napier, p. 404.
[18] "Since the world began was there ever such a man?" *Ibid.,* p. 566. "The struggle between Capo D'Istria and me is like the conflict between a positive and a negative force. . . . But for such a contest what patience is needed." *Ibid.,* p. 571.

and his retirement from the Russian service marked the Czar's complete conversion to reaction.[19]

II

The outbreak of the Greek Insurrection and the task of governing insurgent Greece offered a challenge to the two tenets of Capodistrias's political creed which had most consistently influenced his European policies: his abhorrence of revolution and his hostility to the oligarchic rule of hereditary aristocracies. Educated in Western Europe during the eventful last decade of the eighteenth century,[20] he had absorbed the humanitarianism of the Enlightenment but remained impervious to its philosophic and political radicalism. "He sympathizes," wrote an Austrian diplomat in 1819, "with the sentiments of the age without going so far as to agree with its errors."[21] Regarding himself by birth and achievement as a member of the élite, he was imbued with a sense of responsibility for the welfare of the community and solicitude for the common man. But he doubted the efficacy of popular movements, and the aversion to revolutionary violence which he showed early in his career was intensified by his European experience. His implacable hostility to secret revolutionary societies and the delicacy of his position as a minister of the Czar prompted his vehement rejection of the leadership of *Hetairia Philike*.[22] The outbreak of the Insurrection filled him with misgivings. As a former Venetian subject, a cosmopolite, and a statesman of international reputation he could not feel the need of national liberation with the same passionate urgency as did the Greeks brought

[19] "The Corfiote had the East at heart, and subsequent events proved how consistently he had directed Russian policy in the Levant, and how great was his failure to make it effective.... In the person of Capodistrias, Metternich fought the independence of Russian politics, for Capodistrias stood not only for liberalism but for a Franco-Russian interpretation of the European Concert."—Du Coudray, *op. cit.*, p. 195.

[20] As a student in Padua (1794–98), he witnessed Bonaparte's Italian campaign.

[21] *Diary of Philip von Neumann*, Austrian Chargé d'Affairs in London, Sept. 1, 1819, quoted by Crawley in *The Question of Greek Independence*, p. 233.

[22] In 1816 and 1820. It was after the second rejection that the leadership was offered to A. Ypsilantis.

up under Ottoman rule. At the same time, he was far from indifferent to the plight of Greece and was not averse to striking a blow for her independence. But being essentially a diplomat, he hoped to achieve this aim through diplomatic action, culminating, if necessary, in a Russo-Turkish war, and he was opposed to launching a revolution against the mighty tide of post-Napoleonic reaction.[23] He preferred, in short, to have national independence, like political reform, granted from above rather than wrested by pressure from below.

But though his attitude toward the people was essentially that of an eighteenth-century benevolent monarch, he fancied himself free from the rationalistic delusions of enlightened despotism. He believed that "the statesman who introduces into every country the same institutions regardless of its people's life and culture is as inept and destructive as the physician who prescribes the same diet for every patient, no matter what his constitution and ailment";[24] and he prided himself on governing Greece in accordance with her needs rather than with abstract principles of universal validity. His policies were designed to cater to the needs of those he called "the brave and good people" in order to win the allegiance of the middle and lower classes and to curb the power of "first families, military chieftains, European-minded politicians, and intellectuals generally," who had constituted the ruling class of Greece before and especially during the Insurrection.[25] He envisaged Greece as a nation of small proprietors, and as a first step toward the establishment of this regime he advocated the distribution of the "na-

---

[23] Dragoumes, *Historical Reminiscences*, I, 80, 119. Cf. Finlay, *A History of Greece*, VII, 30–34, and Driault, *Histoire diplomatique de la Grece*, II, 49–51.

[24] This statement of Capodistrias's general position is not incompatible with his memorandum which was delivered to Czar Nicholas early in 1829 by his emissary Count Vaulgari. He was, after all, writing to the champion of absolutism, and as a courtier and a diplomat he stressed his adherence to the monarchical principle, his distrust of democracy, and his detestation of revolutionary violence—on all of which he and the Czar were in agreement. See Letter of Count Voulgaris to Comte de Nesselrode, Poros, Dec. 14, 1828, Annex C–1 with Protocol of Conference, London, March 22, 1829, Doc. No. 17, Great Britain, Foreign Office, *British and Foreign State Papers*, XVII, 151.

[25] G. Skleros, *Contemporary Problems of Hellenism*, p. 81.

tional domain" (that is, the land, buildings, and other property of the Ottoman Government confiscated during the Insurrection) among the discharged veterans of the Revolution.[26] That this was a wise and imperatively needed program of national reconstruction is indisputable. Yet the statesman who conceived it, though he professed to be a hater of doctrinaires, brought to its execution a stubbornly doctrinaire temper aggravated by the meticulousness of a conscientious bureaucrat. Like the most "enlightened" of the eighteenth-century monarchs, he ignored traditional leadership and attempted to ride rough shod over vested interests. Ever mindful of his European eminence, he looked down with haughty condescension upon those who could lay claim to any sort of eminence in Greece. Toward those proud men who had been the leaders of the insurgent nation for seven years and whose co-operation was indispensable in the organization of the new state, he often adopted a tone of didactic omniscience and self-righteousness; and he inflicted upon them the petty tyranny and the incompetence of his brothers and protégés to whose glaring inadequacy he was pathetically blind.[27] Because his efforts to establish orderly and frugal government through an efficient bureaucracy were impeded by the inertia of strongly entrenched oligarchs, the truculence of military chieftains, the hair splitting of would-be political theorists, and the sniping of journalists and other intellectuals,[28] he allowed his initial prejudice against these groups to crystallize into indiscriminate and undisguised hostility. "He called," writes Tricoupis, who had been his Secretary of State, "the notables, Turks masquerading under Christian names; the military chieftains, brigands; the Phanariots, vessels of Satan; and the intellectuals, fools. Only the peasants and the artisans did

---

[26] A. Andreades, *Studies in Public Economy*, p. 24.

[27] He wrote of his brothers Agostino and Viaro, and of his protégé Gennatas: "The more I can have of their ability, the more I can hope for a little order in this country." Letter to Mustoxidi, April 26, 1828, J. Capodistrias, *Correspondence*, II, 36.

[28] Many of these were disappointed officeholders, for in his passion for economy he reduced the seven ministries and 185 secretaryships of the central Government to one Secretary of State and eleven clerks. See Andreades, *op. cit.*, p. 28.

he consider worthy of his love and protection, and he openly declared that his administration was conducted solely for their benefit." He was often betrayed by his hostility against the notables into acts of injustice, such as his rebuke to the brothers Coundouriotis, who had impoverished themselves in order to finance the Insurrection, for their allegedly small contribution to the founding of a national bank;[29] and he was driven to commit disastrous indiscretions, as when he assured the king of France that the Greek people longed to be delivered permanently from "the tyranny of the primates and the military chieftains."[30] This attitude drove to sullen opposition numerous influential leaders who had initially acknowledged his authority and bowed to his higher competence. Abetted by the diplomatic agents of Great Britain and France, who fought Capodistrias as the reputed catspaw of Russia, these leaders did not shrink from armed rebellion against his heroic effort to habituate insurgent Greece to the rule of law and to organize a central government capable of enforcing its writ. The insurrection of Hydra and Maina, which was the immediate cause of his assassination,[31] might have been averted if he had known how to avoid adding insult to injury; in other words, if, instead of ostentatiously exalting the lowly and abasing the proud, he had stooped to conciliate those whose ascendancy was threatened by his policies.

But while Capodistrias had a rather low opinion of the leaders of the Insurrection, he did not underestimate the difficulties against which they had had to contend. Much as he deprecated their constitution-mongering, he approved its basic aim—the organization of a unitary state and a strong central government. He recognized that failure to achieve this aim was due, not to the representative institutions of insurgent Greece, but to the

---

[29] Message to the Panhellenion, March 11, 1828, Capodistrias, *Correspondence*, I, 425. Letter to L. Coundouriotis, March 14, 1828, *ibid.*, p. 484.

[30] Letter to Count Loverdo for transmission to Charles X, Dec. 15, 1828, *ibid.*, II, 454.

[31] He was assassinated on Oct. 9, 1831, by the son and the brother of Peter Mainiol, chief of the Mainiol Clan.

financial insolvency and consequent impotence of the central government, which enabled the local oligarchs to preserve their power.[32] His objection to the Constitution of Troezene was, not that it was democratic, but that (*a*) it provided a weak executive, and (*b*) it had been framed without regard to the fact that independence had not yet been won and before the boundaries of the new State were determined. In order of their urgency, he conceived the tasks confronting Greek statesmanship to be: (*a*) the liquidation of the war, with full independence and the most favorable territorial settlement; (*b*) the economic and social reconstruction of the country; and (*c*) the determination of its definitive form of government.[33] While he concerned himself with the first and second of these tasks, he proceeded to organize an admittedly provisional regime designed to promote "orderly government" and to serve as part of the Greek people's apprenticeship toward full-fledged constitutionalism. He discerned that it was essential to the mediating powers that Greece should become an element of international order and stability; and he realized that a monarchy, largely because it would be deemed to fulfill this condition, would secure for Greece the most favorable territorial settlement.[34] He insisted, however, that the monarchy should be constitutional.[35] He repeatedly urged the candidacy of Prince

---

[32] Circular of May 29, 1829, Capodistrias, *Correspondence*, III, 150.

[33] Instructions to Committee on the Constitution, Feb. 16, 1830, *ibid.*, III, 477.

[34] Preamble to the Decree of July 23 (Aug. 5), 1829, of the Fourth National Assembly, Mamoukas, *Documents Relating to the Greek Renaissance*, XI, 57. See also closing message of Capodistrias to the Fourth National Assembly, Aug. 6 (19), 1829, *ibid.*, p. 125.

[35] To a deputation of Hydriots who waited on him to urge the drawing up of a definitive constitution in accordance with principles of the Revolutionary assemblies, Capodistrias replied: "*Of course,* but that is not an *urgent* matter. Do you take me for a Turk? Am I an enemy of constitutions? I desire as much as you that Greece should be governed by a constitution. I have said and repeated it often. But is this the time to bring it up? The existence of Greece depends entirely on her foreign policy, and it is to her relations with the powers that she must devote her attention."—Driault, *op. cit.*, II, 9. While there was no explicit mandate for establishment of a monarchy, there was explicit mandate from the Senate for choice of a monarch after Leopold's renunciation (Protocol of Conference, London, Sept. 26, 1831). On the other hand, see Voulgaris's re-

Leopold of Coburg on the British Government;[36] and long before the London Conference announced its decision, he laid down a general line of policy for the Prince to follow and instructed him "by a formal act to come to an agreement with the nation on the principles which should govern the administration of the state."[37] He pursued this line vigorously in his correspondence with the Prince after February 3, 1830. He began his reply to the Prince's announcement that he had accepted the offer of the powers by protesting against the refusal of the London Conference to admit the Greek Government to its negotiations and its apparent determination to impose the settlement embodied in the Protocols of February 3, 1830, rather than allow the Greek people to accept it by orderly constitutional procedure. He drew the Prince's attention to the fact that the Protocols did not contain "a single word about the public law of the Greeks"; and he offered as alternative explanations of this omission either that the powers held the view that the monarch "absorbs and concentrates in his person" all the rights of his people or that it had been left to Leopold's initiative to recognize these rights by a solemn declaration before his accession. He added significantly that he had held out the promise of such a declaration to the Senate and the people, who had been disturbed by the silence of the Protocols on the constitutional issue; and he ended by advising Leopold to announce immediately that he intended to govern constitutionally, to invite the participation of the people in framing a definitive constitution, and to base it, in accordance with the decree of

---

port to Czar Nicholas, which would seem to raise doubts about the sincerity of Capodistrias's constitutionalism (see Note 24, *supra*).

[36] He first spoke guardedly to Stratford Canning at Poros about a German prince. He spoke to Canning again of a German prince and, after the report was signed, disclosed his meaning. "The person whom he designs for his German prince is no other than Prince Leopold, and he has assured me in confidence that the Prince is willing and that he had sounded H.R.H. when in England." Canning to Aberdeen, *Stratford Canning Papers*, 20, as cited by Crawley, *op. cit.*, pp. 143, 149. Canning reported to Alexander, Capodistrias's expressed intention to retire, *ibid.*, p. 150.

[37] Memorandum to Leopold, May 30, 1829, Capodistrias, *Correspondence*, III, 154.

the fourth National Convention, on the principles laid down by the three constituent assemblies of the Revolution.[38]

It has been asserted that Capodistrias's insistence on the need of a constitution and the generally gloomy picture of conditions in Greece which he presented to Leopold were intended to frighten him into declining the offer of the London Conference. It has been pointed out that, though Capodistrias had been the first to suggest to the powers Leopold's candidacy,[39] when it seemed that Greece would be no more than a principality under Ottoman suzerainty, he reversed his stand after the independence of Greece had been recognized because "he knew that he would have less influence over a sovereign than over a vassal Prince." The fact that Leopold eventually renounced the Greek throne and that his action was undeniably influenced by the unfavorable reports he had received from the highest authority in Greece,[40] can be adduced as strong *ex post facto* evidence against Capodistrias's sincerity. His harping on the popular demand for a constitution to be framed in collaboration with a national assembly must have had a particularly deterrent effect on a prince who considered himself "at full liberty to give or not to give such institutions as, compatible with a monarchy," he would in time "find necessary for the welfare of the new state."[41] On the other hand, it may be urged on behalf of Capodistrias that his communications to Leopold were less pessimistic than his private letters to intimate friends;[42] that his account of conditions in Greece and of the state of public opinion was

---

[38] Letter (Particular) of Capodistrias to Leopold, March 25 (April 6), 1830, Enclosure B with Letter to Leopold to the Plenipotentiaries of the Three Allied Courts, May 15, 1830, Doc. No. 39, B.F.S.P., XVII, 494–96.

[39] Crawley, *op. cit.*, p. 179.

[40] See Leopold's letter of renunciation to the Plenipotentiaries of the Three Allied Courts, May 21, 1830, Doc. No. 42, B.F.S.P., XVII, 500.

[41] Leopold's memorandum to Wellington, Feb. 9, 1830, Doc. No. 7, *ibid.*, p. 459. Cf. Doc. No. XLVIII in Strupp, *op. cit.*, pp. 101–104.

[42] Letter of Eynard to Lord Stuart de Rothesay defending Capodistrias, enclosed with Letter of de Rothesay to Aberdeen, May 28, 1830, Doc. No. 4, B.F.S.P., XVII, 519. See also Capodistrias's letters to Eynard, April 6 and 24, 1830, sub-enclosures A and B, *ibid.*, pp. 522, 524. Capodistrias: "Je démontre à S.A.R. que ses devoirs, comme ses intérêts les plus chers, doivent l'engager à se rendre sans aucun retard en Grèce." (Especially in order to supervise long and arduous task of delimitation.)

supported by the testimony of disinterested foreign observers;[43] that far from desiring to influence Leopold adversely, he regarded the Coburg prince's accession as an all but accomplished fact, addressed him as his sovereign "who had definitely and positively accepted the crown," repeatedly urged him to hasten his arrival, and begged him, in the meantime, for a kingly gesture that would strengthen his own position;[44] finally, that his reports about popular dissatisfaction with the decisions of the London Conference, particularly with the silence of the Protocols on the constitutional issue, were fully confirmed by the resident envoys of the three powers.[45]

III

But when all is said, the most valid test of Capodistrias's sincerity is provided by his own record. In his recommendations to Prince Leopold he upheld the sovereignty of the nation, defended the people's right to be consulted with regard to their fundamental law, and advocated constitutional and representative government. To what extent was this precept consistent with his example, that is, with the policies he pursued as president of Greece?

His first act was to suspend the Constitution, which had been drafted by the third National Convention, and within whose limitations it was the intent of its framers that he should conduct his government.

This decision was prompted primarily by the conviction that the urgent tasks which confronted him—the negotiation of a favorable peace and the internal reconstruction of the country—could not be carried out under a constitution which had been deliberately fashioned to curb the executive.[46] But even if he

[43] Letter of Fabrequette, paymaster of the Greek army in Modon, to Eynard, April 26, 1830, sub-enclosure C with Letter of de Rothesay to Aberdeen, May 28, 1830, Doc. No. 4, *ibid.*, p. 525.

[44] Letters (two) from Capodistrias to Leopold, A and B, May 24, 1830, attached to Protocol, London, July 26, 1830, *ibid.*, pp. 615, 617. These letters were written three days after Leopold had made known his decision to decline the offer of the powers.

[45] Resident Envoys' Report, April, 1830, marked A, with Protocol, London, July 1, 1830, Doc. No. 33, *ibid.*, pp. 606–11.

[46] See p. 51, *supra*. Also Capodistrias's answer to 28th question of the Envoys, Mamoukas, *op. cit.*, XI, 327–36.

had been willing to acquiesce in the restrictions which hedged in his office, he could not have governed within the framework of an organic law whose fundamental premise had no *de facto* or *de jure* validity. For both the Constitution (Article CXXV) and the presidential oath attached to it assumed that the Insurrection had already attained its goal and solemnly charged the president with "the defense and preservation" of national independence at a time when the utmost that had been conceded to Greece was tributary autonomy under Ottoman suzerainty.[47] Being a stickler for legality, Capodistrias would probably have been satisfied, under the circumstances, with orderly and partial revision designed to expand the powers of the president and to remove the glaring discrepancy between his duties and the international status of Greece. But since no provision had been made for an amending process, he secured from the legislature immediate passage of an Enabling Act setting up a "provisional" government, subject to ratification by a national assembly which he promised to convoke within two months.[48] He implicitly admitted the unconstitutionality of this procedure,[49] but invoked the exigencies of a national emergency, stressed the fact that his provisional government was founded on the principles laid down by the three assemblies of the Revolution, and undertook, by the terms of the presidential oath, drafted by himself, to govern in accordance with these principles—a commitment which he repeated in all subsequent state papers pertaining to constitutional issues.[50]

Granted that the emergency regime established by Capodis-

---

[47] Article 125 of the Troezene Constitution; and presidential oath attached to the constitution. B.S.F.P., XV, 1077, 1081.

[48] The presidential proclamation was dated Jan. 20 (Feb. 2), 1828. The convocation of the Assembly was set for April. *Ibid.*, p. 1087.

[49] He repeatedly expressed regret that they had not been authorized to vote amendments to the constitution. Article 94 expressly forbade the legislature to amend the constitution, and this probihition was reiterated by Section 2 of a constitutional resolution of the Third National Convention, which enjoined the Legislature and the Government "from legislating or acting against the constitution." Mamoukas, *op. cit.*, IX, 151.

[50] The President's Message to the Legislature, Jan. 17 (30), 1828; resolution of the Legislature, Jan. 18 (31), 1828; the President's Proclamation to the Nation, Jan. 20 (Feb. 2), 1828. *Ibid.*, X, 38–47.

trias was imperatively needed and that it was set up with strict regard to such legal procedure as was available, to what extent was the claim warranted that it was based on the liberal and democratic principles enunciated by the assemblies of the Revolution? An answer to this question is supplied by (*a*) the provisions of the Enabling Act of January 30, 1828, (*b*) the amendments made to it by the fourth National Convention, (*c*) the President's views on the franchise and on electoral procedure, and (*d*) the changes he introduced into the system of provincial administration and local self-government.

The Enabling Act of January 30, 1828, dissolved the legislature which had been elected in accordance with the Constitution of Troezene and transferred its powers to the President and a body of twenty-seven members appointed by him and "participating with him in the work and responsibility of government."[51] This body, which was called the *Panhellenion,* was divided into three sections—finance, interior, and national defense—and performed both legislative and administrative functions; and though it could only act in an advisory capacity, the independence of its members and Capodistrias's scrupulous adherence to the procedure of consultation and adjustment made it a far from pliant instrument in the President's hands. Contact and co-ordination with the *Panhellenion* were secured through the secretaries of the three sections, who were appointed by the President; while the administration of the various departments was entrusted to decidedly subordinate ministers headed by the Secretary of State. This provisional regime may be fairly described, then, as a presidential dictatorship which violated two principles that had been embodied in all three constitutions of the Revolution—the separation of powers and the primacy of the legislature over the executive. But it was a dictatorship of delegated powers, limited in duration and accountable to a national assembly on the expiration of its mandate.

That such was Capodistrias's conception of his administration is evident from the proceedings of the fourth National

[51] Article II, Section 1, of the Enabling Act, *ibid.*

Assembly, which met at Argos on July 23, 1829, after repeated postponements. He submitted to the Assembly, through the appropriate ministers, detailed reports of the work of his government in the fields of foreign affairs, public finance, internal organization, and national defense.[52] After these reports had been examined by *ad hoc* committees, the Assembly endorsed the President's record and proceeded to renew his mandate. This additional grant of powers was made in the form of thirteen resolutions which directed the President to deal with as many specific questions—from foreign policy to the preservation of the archæological treasures of the nation—and laid down the general principles that should in each case govern his action.[53] The second of these resolutions dealt with the constitutional issue. It accepted the President's request for prolongation of the provisional regime on the ground that the main reason for its existence—the undetermined international status of Greece—was still valid;[54] it amended the Enabling Act of January 30, 1828, with a view to modifying the machinery of the provisional government; it formulated the basic principles of the definitive Constitution and directed the President to draft it in collaboration with the Senate (the successor of the *Panhellenion*) ; and it prorogued itself after a short session of less than a month,[55] but stipulated that it should be reconvoked in order to ratify the Constitution and the final peace settlement.[56]

The revision of the provisional government, obviously inspired by the President, was intended to make it more efficient and pliable. The *Panhellenion*, which had proved recalcitrant on several occasions, was replaced by a Senate with the same number of members, of whom six were appointed directly and the remaining twenty-one selected by the President from a list of sixty-three candidates drawn up by the Assembly and representing proportionately the three main sections of Greece.[57]

[52] *Ibid.*, XI, 26; 30–33, 223, 383–404, 465–547.
[53] *Ibid.*, pp. 139–200.
[54] Resolution No. II, *ibid.*, p. 144. President's Farewell Address, *ibid.*, p. 126.
[55] July 11 (24) to Aug. 6 (19), 1829.
[56] Resolutions Nos. I and II, *ibid.*, pp. 139–48; No. XIII, *ibid.*, p. 197.
[57] The President's Message to the Assembly (Hellenic State Document [state papers of the Greek Government, hereafter cited as H.S.D.] No. 13594), Aug. 2 (15), 1829, *ibid.*, p. 825.

THE CAPODISTRIAN DICTATORSHIP

Unlike its predecessor, this body was vested with clearly defined powers. All money bills and all measures dealing with the disposal of the "national domain" were subject to its approval. On the other hand, while it had the right to be consulted on all other measures, except strictly administrative ordinances, its consent was not essential to their enactment. In case of disagreement they were promulgated as executive decrees and thereby became law subject to final ratification by the next National Assembly.[58]

After re-emphasizing that the definitive constitution must not deviate from the principles which inspired the constitutions of the Revolution, the Assembly instructed the President and the Senate to include provisions dealing with citizenship, naturalization, the franchise, and electoral procedure; to create a judiciary, with life-tenure for the judges, and a bicameral legislature; and, significantly enough, to fashion the executive "in the spirit which dictated the acts of Troezene," subject to such modifications as might be rendered necessary by the final settlement of the international status of Greece.[59] The President accepted these instructions and pledged himself, pending reconvocation of the Assembly, to "work unremittingly in order to prepare the nation for the enjoyment of stable well-being under constitutional government."[60]

With regard to Capodistrias's views on the franchise, a distinction must be made between the principles he applied to his own provisional regime and those he intended to embody in the definitive constitution of Greece. The assemblies of the Revolution were elected by an approximation of universal manhood suffrage and a system of indirect election whereby the initial voters chose the so-called first degree electors, who in turn voted for representatives.[61] Invited by the President to formulate the electoral law more clearly, the *Panhellenion* submitted a series of amendments which proposed to disfranchise *"heter-*

[58] Resolution No. II, Articles 2–7, *ibid.*, p. 147.
[59] Resolution No. II, Part 2, *ibid.*
[60] The President's Farewell Address, *ibid.*, p. 126.
[61] Law No. XVII, *ibid.*, III, 69. Cf. p. 54, *supra;* and H.S.D. No. 7495, *ibid.*, X, 50.

ochthonous" (non-native) Greeks, domestic servants, and the upper clergy, subject first-degree electors to steep property qualifications, raise them still further for representatives, and make persons with a prison record ineligible in either capacity.[62] The President rejected these proposals, pleading his lack of authority "to make any laws whatsoever, and particularly a law designed to abridge the right to vote, which the Greek people flatter themselves that they have enjoyed heretofore without any restrictions."[63] The *Panhellenion* retorted that acceptance of this *ultra vires* argument would invalidate all the legislative measures passed by the provisional government since its inception; but it hastened to uphold the validity of these laws by citing the provisions of the Enabling Act of January 30, 1828, which empowered the President to issue not only executive ordinances but legislative decrees as well "on all matters that have not yet been provided for by law."[64] Though the President's position was theoretically untenable, he had his way on the substance of the controversy, after a protracted debate, with only one minor concession; and the elections were conducted by what amounted to manhood suffrage (all citizens who had completed their twenty-fifth year being entitled to vote), and with no property qualifications for either first-degree electors or members of the Assembly.[65]

Capodistrias's defense of manhood suffrage was largely inspired by political expediency. He had been consistently opposed to the doctrine of natural rights, and he felt toward the people the philosopher-king's solicitude for, rather than the democrat's faith in, the common man. Recognizing the demo-

---

[62] Also beggars, insane persons, and criminals, Panhellenion Series Doc. No. 12, *ibid.*, pp. 53–60.

[63] The President's reply to the Panhellenion, H.S.D. No. 8874, *ibid.*, p. 74.

[64] The Panhellenion's reply to the President, Panhellenion Series Doc. No. 13, *ibid.*, p. 77.

[65] He accepted the Panhellenion's proposal that persons imprisoned for civil offenses should be released on bail in order to vote or, if need be, perform their duties as electors and members. See Proceedings of the Panhellenion and Correspondence with the President, *ibid.*, pp. 80–90 (including footnotes). H.S.D. Nos. 10049, 10050, 10051, *ibid.*, pp. 90–100. Instructions to Provincial Authorities, *ibid.*, pp. 101–7.

cratic and equalitarian temper of the Greek people, he attempted to consolidate his regime on an alliance with the middle class, the artisans, and the peasants; and he conceived the electoral system as the most effective device for curbing the power of the ruling oligarchy. But because the political immaturity of the Greeks was just as axiomatic with him as the ineptitude of their leaders, he was forever spreading over the untutored democracy the protecting wings of enlightened and benevolent government. Thus, while he opposed the least curtailment of the franchise and was even inclined to dispense with indirect elections as a mere formality,[66] he insisted on such meticulous supervision and guidance of the voters as to lend color to his opponents' charge that he was aiming at government control of the elections. He alienated irretrievably the orthodox constitutionalists and caused the resignation of Tricoupis, his Secretary of State, by condoning the election to the Assembly of instructed members who had received an imperative mandate from their constituents to endorse his past course and to approve his plans for the future.[67] With the ostensible intention of maintaining order, but aiming in reality to deprive the local oligarchs of their influence over elections, he proposed that the electoral colleges, that is, the meetings of the first degree electors, should be presided over by government officials; and it was only after a long debate with the *Panhellenion* that he consented to a compromise whereby the chairmanship of the electoral college was entrusted to one of their members selected by the government.[68]

On the other hand, Capodistrias's views concerning the franchise provisions of the definitive constitution were derived from his conception of the most desirable social organization for Greece. While he believed that, since the duty to fight confers the right to vote, no individual or class should have been dis-

---

[66] The President's Circular to Provincial Authorities, H.S.D. No. 12369, *ibid.*, p. 117.
[67] Dragoumes, *op. cit.*, I, 82.
[68] Proceedings of the Panhellenion, Jan. 25 (Feb. 7), 1829, Mamoukas, *op. cit.*, X, 80 (footnote). The President's Circular of March 4 (17), 1829, *ibid.*, p. 101.

franchised during the Insurrection, he wanted to make property the decisive qualification in time of peace. But he was profoundly dissatisfied with the existing distribution of property. Precisely because he was convinced that only those who had a material stake in the country should exercise the positive functions of citizenship, he envisaged Greece as a nation of landed proprietors. He therefore invited the collaboration of the Senate in framing the necessary legislation for the immediate distribution of the national domain in order to give political independence "to the vast majority of the citizens of the state."[69]

Capodistrias's "provisional" system of provincial administration was an attempt to graft the newly created organs of centralized control upon the existing institutions of local self-government, that is, the communal and the district councils of elders. The communal councils varied in size, consisting of one elder for every hundred families, but not exceeding a maximum membership of four; and while they were elected by all the qualified voters of the commune, only those who "were most heavily taxed" and had completed their thirty-fifth year were eligible to them. The district councils were formed by combining the council of the capital city of the district with representatives of its rural sections elected by the communal councils.[70] These arrangements did not differ materially from the traditional system of local self-government which the Revolution had inherited from the Ottoman regime. Nor did Capodistrias innovate when he attached these elective bodies, both in an advisory and in an administrative capacity, to the prefects appointed by the central Government;[71] for this arrangement had been adumbrated in the "Provisional Electoral Law" of November 22, 1822, and endorsed by the third National Convention.[72] Moreover, while repugnant to orthodox exponents of local autonomy, this combination was both economical (since it re-

[69] H.S.D. No. 1747, Decree of April 16 (29), 1828, *ibid.*, XI, 395.
[70] H.S.D. No. 1883, Decree of April 19 (May 2), 1828, *ibid.*, p. 395*n*.
[71] See pp. 55–56, *supra*. Resolution of May 1 (14), 1827. Proceedings of the Third National Convention, *ibid.*, IX, 121.
[72] Mendelssohn-Bartholdy, *op. cit.*, II, 248.

duced to a minimum the provincial officials employed by the central Government) and conducive to administrative cohesion and stability. Less defensible was the dominant part played by government officials in the election of both communal and district councils. Enjoying the right to preside over the electoral assemblies and to supervise the lists of eligible candidates, they tended to substitute governmental favoritism and pressure for those local influences which, however abhorrent to Capodistrias, were indispensable to the proper functioning of local self-government.

The main points made in the course of this survey may now be briefly summarized. Capodistrias distinguished clearly between his own administration, which he regarded as an interregnum, and the permanent form of government of independent Greece. Because the former was essentially an emergency government, he organized it as a legal dictatorship, which derived its authority from and was accountable to the representatives of the people, but was governed by successive mandates rather than under constant parliamentary supervision and control. Nevertheless, he deprecated authoritarian government as a permanent regime; and he believed that the nation should seek to safeguard its future, not by surrendering its sovereign rights, but by exercising them through representative institutions. Hence he envisaged radical economic reforms designed to provide the material foundation for political democracy. And while he initiated or inspired most of the measures of the consultative bodies which functioned during his administration, he adhered scrupulously to legal methods and parliamentary procedure in order to habituate the Greek people to the processes of free yet lawful government.

Chapter Four

THE FORFEITURE OF SOVEREIGNTY

I

THROUGHOUT the long struggle for independence insurgent Greece was internally sovereign. Her government, though palpably deficient by all the essential tests of governmental efficacy, left nothing to be desired with respect to its origins. It was the expression of the general will, insofar as the general will could be ascertained and expressed under the circumstances. The third and most elaborate of the constitutions purporting to embody the will of the nation was set aside by President Capodistrias mainly because its validity was contingent upon full independence, which had not yet been achieved, that is, internationally recognized. This condition was fulfilled two years later. But the same diplomatic instrument—the Protocols of February 3, 1830—which made Greece independent, namely, sovereign with relation to other states, delivered a blow at her internal sovereignty by prescribing the form of government of the new state and by dictating to it on important aspects of its public law. The London Conference of Ambassadors, arrogating to itself the constituent power of the Greek nation, decided that its government should be monarchical; it conferred on the Catholic Church in Greece—its bishops, its property, and its missions, "the rights and privileges which it had enjoyed (in the Ottoman Empire) under the patronage of the Kings of France"; and, actuated by "benevolent solicitude" for Greece and the desire to save her from the evils of religious dissension, it decreed that "all the subjects of the new state, whatever their religion, shall be admitted to all public positions, functions and honours and treated on the basis of complete equality . . . in all their religious, civil and political relations."[1] What warrant was there for this action; to what extent did it impair the sovereignty of the new state; and what were its consequences for the constitutional development of Greece?

The intervention of the three protecting powers in the Greek Insurrection can be traced to the "Act of Submission" by which a representative but not duly constituted group of notables invoked the "exclusive protection of Great Britain" in order to save Greece from the fury of the Turco-Egyptian invaders and from the putative designs of the other powers.[2] While refusing for cogent reasons to accept this complete surrender of sovereignty, George Canning, the British Foreign Secretary, eventually deduced from it an appeal for mediation and held out the promise that "there might be a point in the contest when Great Britain would promote a fair and safe compromise."[3] The St. Petersburg Protocol of April 4, 1826, associated Russia in this mediatory action which was to be based on the recognition of Greece as an autonomous state under Ottoman suzerainty.[4] The adherence of France was secured by the London Treaty of July 6, 1827, which, after reiterating that the mediation was undertaken at the urgent request of the Greek people, reaffirmed the terms of the St. Petersburg Protocol.[5]

In the meantime, the Greek appeal for mediation had been repeated more explicitly and authoritatively. The third National Assembly, duly instructed by Sir Stratford Canning, British Ambassador in Constantinople, empowered him to "negotiate and conclude a settlement that should satisfy the honor and the in-

---

[1] Protocol (3) of Plenipotentiaries of Great Britain, France, and Russia, London, Feb. 3, 1830, Doc. No. 25, Great Britain, Foreign Office, *British and Foreign State Papers*, XVII, 202–3. Cf. Sir James Wycliffe Headlam-Morley, *Studies in Diplomatic History*, pp. 126–30.

[2] Act of the Provisional Government, July 24, 1825, B.F.S.P., XII, 904–6.

[3] As quoted by Crawley in *The Question of Greek Independence*, p. 47.

[4] Protocol (1) of British and Russian Plenipotentiaries, St. Petersburg, April 4, 1826, B.F.S.P., XIV, 629–32. Also Doc. No. I in Strupp, ed., *La Situation internationale de la Grèce*, pp. 3–4.

[5] Treaty for the Pacification of Greece between Great Britain, France and Russia, London, July 6, 1827, B.F.S.P., XIV, 632–39. Also Doc. No. II in Strupp, ed., *op. cit.*, pp. 5–7.

terests of the Greek nation and be commensurate with its sacrifices for freedom";[6] and while the Assembly's instructions to its diplomatic commission contained the maximum territorial and economic demands of Greece, they accepted the political terms laid down by the mediating powers, namely, Ottoman suzerainty and, in token thereof, payment of tribute.[7] It is true that these instructions were inferentially contradicted by the assumption of complete independence which was basic to the constitution subsequently framed by the same Assembly. But this inconsistency was removed when the authorized spokesmen of the Greek Government accepted the powers' offer of an armistice within the terms of the London Treaty.[8] Under the status of vassalage which insurgent Greece thus accepted as the basis of her "pacification," her freedom to determine her form of government was limited by the rights of the suzerain power. Inasmuch as the retention of the Ottoman connection impaired both the international independence and the internal self-determination of the new state, the mandate authorizing the protecting powers to negotiate peace may be said to have involved a surrender of the constituent power which the Greek people had exercised throughout the Insurrection.

The British, French, and Russian Governments proceeded on this tacit assumption. Their ambassadors in Constantinople, who were sent to Greece with instructions to submit recommendations for implementing the Treaty of July 6, 1827, concerned themselves not only with the territorial, economic, and financial terms of the settlement, but also with the political regime to be established in the autonomous state. They regarded President Capodistrias's government as temporary, took for granted the right of the powers to determine its definitive successor, and believed that Greece could not "ursurp the in-

[6] Finlay, *History of Greece,* VII, 11. Footnote 1 states that the Decree and the letter to Canning are given by Mamoukas, *Documents Relating to the Greek Renaissance,* IV, 94, 132.

[7] Finlay, *loc. cit.* See also Article II, Treaty, London, July 6, 1827, B.F.S.P., XIV, 635.

[8] Proclamation of the Provisional Government of Greece accepting the Armistice, Aug. 21, 1827, B.F.S.P., XIV, 1048.

itiative of the Courts," since she depended on their good will for her existence and restoration to statehood. What should be the permanent political regime of the new state? The ambassador's approach to this question was primarily international.

Assuming that the aim of the mediating powers was "to make the tranquillity of Greece one of the elements of the tranquillity of Europe," they urged the need of "giving the Greeks the indispensable means of achieving that degree of internal strength" which was essential to appeasement. They made a keen diagnosis of the political instability of the Revolution and pointed out that the Greeks turned to Capodistrias only after they had become convinced that it was impossible to form a government of native leaders without raising against it "a coalition of numberless rival powers." And they concluded that the cultural legacy of Ottoman rule, the geographical and climatic variety of the country, and the resultant "diversity of local interests" made it imperative that the new state should be founded on the hereditary principle which was the best guarantee of its prosperity and independence, and hence "a lasting safeguard of the tranquillity of Europe."[9]

Moreover, the ambassadors argued, hereditary monarchy would reduce the interference of the suzerain power to a minimum. Whereas under an elective magistracy the Ottoman Government might claim the right to veto every presidential election, under a hereditary regime it would only exercise the right of investiture whenever there occurred a change of dynasty, and would thus "participate in the devolution of power" at much rarer intervals. Finally, with regard to the probable attitude of the people toward a monarchy, the ambassadors called attention to the fact that the Greeks had been accustomed to municipal and cultural autonomy under Ottoman rule and to representative government throughout the Insurrection, and concluded that the proposed hereditary regime would add to its stability if it were tempered by representative institutions.[10]

[9] Annex "F," "Suzerainty," Protocol, Poros, Dec. 12, 1828, *ibid.*, XVII, 428–31.
[10] *Ibid.*, p. 430.

The London Conference, by the Protocol of March 22, 1829, endorsed these recommendations and decided that the government of Greece should be "assimilated as much as possible to monarchical forms."[11] But the situation was altered by the outcome of the Russo-Turkish war, which not only compelled the Ottoman Government to accept the Treaty of July 6, 1827, and the Protocol of March 22, 1829, and to "subscribe entirely" to all future decisions of the London Conference,[12] but helped to convert the British Cabinet to the principle of full independence for Greece provided it was accompanied by a niggardly territorial settlement.[13] Yet despite her progress from vassalage to sovereignty, Greece was still denied the right to determine her form of government. By a very broad construction of the mandate they had received from the Greek people, the mediating powers decided that the new state should be a monarchy, because "only a monarchical and hereditary government offered the guarantees of stability" and, hence, the assurance of "pacification." This assumption of "implied powers," however tenuous may have been its legal warrant, was doubtless the most expedient course politically and was amply justified by the decisive part played by the three Governments in the creation of the new state. The Protocols of February 3, 1830, were accompanied by a stern reminder that "Greece owed its life to the assistance lavished upon it by the three powers"; that they had "liberated, taken it under their immediate protection, and saved it from inevitable ruin"; and that these services entitled them to "positive rights and to complete deference" on the part of the Greek nation.[14] Finally, the protecting powers could claim with justice that they had ascertained the needs and the

---

[11] "Suzerainty," Protocol, London, March 22, 1829, *ibid.*, XVI, 1097. Also Doc. No. XXXVIII in Strupp, *op. cit.*, p. 85.

[12] Annex "B," Declaration of the Porte, Sept. 9, 1829, Protocol (1), London, Feb. 3, 1830, Doc. No. 23, B.F.S.P., XVII, 195.

[13] Article I, Protocol (1), London, Feb. 3, 1830, Doc. No. 23, *ibid.*, p. 192, and Annex "H," Instructions to the Plenipotentiaries of the Three Courts in Constantinople, *ibid.*, pp. 199–200. The latter also Doc. No. XLVII in Strupp, *op. cit.*, p. 98. Cf. Crawley, *op. cit.*, pp. 167, 173.

[14] Annex "I," Instructions to the Residents of the Three Courts in Greece, Protocol (1), London, Feb. 3, 1830, Doc. No. 23, B.F.S.P., XVII, 200.

public sentiment of Greece through an inquiry conducted on the spot by their envoys; and that their decision on the question of the regime, while dictated by their pronounced monarchist predilections, was not contrary to the national will.

II

This cannot be said, however, of the failure of the protecting powers to impose, in accordance with the recommendations of their envoys, a minimum of constitutional limitations on the monarchy which their will had called into existence. The Government of insurgent Greece, such as it was, had been organized and conducted on the theory that sovereignty resides in the nation; that the primary manifestation of sovereignty is the exercise of the constituent power with a view of providing the state with a written constitution; and that the main object of a constitution should be to reconcile authority with liberty—to organize the power of the state and, at the same time, to safeguard the rights of the citizen and to make government amenable to popular control through representative institutions. Despite the wide gap between the theory and the realities of government in the midst of war and invasion, internecine strife, financial insolvency, and foreign intervention, the tradition of constitutionalism which developed during the Insurrection was a definite reality and should not have been ignored by those who undertook to dictate the fundamental law of the new state. Paradoxically enough, the defense of this tradition devolved upon President Capodistrias, whose unorthodox constitutional policy had driven the constitutionalist party to fierce opposition.[15] The solicitude for the sovereign rights of the Greek people, which characterized his foreign policy, was largely prompted no doubt by what he understood to be the exigencies of a diplomatic struggle which he had to wage while completely deprived of force—the indispensable complement of diplomacy.

[15] Annex "F," Memorandum of the Provisional Government of Greece to the Residents of the Three Courts, April 16, 1830, Protocol, London, May 14, 1830, Doc. No. 29, *ibid.*, pp. 218–220. See also Finlay, *op. cit.*, VII, 32–33; 40 ff., and chap. iii, *supra.*

He must have known, for instance, that the participation of an insurgent people, who had begged for mediation, in the deliberations of the mediating powers was juridically inadmissible and politically impracticable; and that, hence, his "reiterated requests" for the admittance of Greece to the London Conference could not be granted.[16] He must also have known that at a time when the mediating powers were congratulating themselves on having saved Greece and preserved the peace of Europe, they would not be greatly impressed by the fact that the fourth National Convention had forbidden acceptance of the peace settlement by the President without previous ratification by the representatives of the Greek people.[17] But when he affirmed the people's claim to the constituent power, he was on much firmer ground. He pleaded with Prince Leopold to recognize this claim by promising to govern within the limits of a constitution framed with the collaboration of the nation and in accordance with the principles promulgated by the constituent assemblies of the Revolution.[18] He doubtless inspired the thinly veiled protest of the Senate, which, after announcing that it accepted the powers' decision concerning the regime because it was dictated by considerations of "high policy," expressed the hope that Prince Leopold would "validate the national liberties which Greece has consecrated in four national assemblies and which she considers as necessary and precious as her very existence as a nation."[19] Finally, he pointed out to the resident envoys of the three powers that "the absolute silence" of the Protocols on the constitutional issue would "compromise

---

[16] Letter (Confidential) of Capodistrias to Leopold, April 6, 1830, Inclosure "A" with Letter of Leopold to the Plenipotentiaries of the Three Allied Courts, May 15, 1830, Doc. No. 39, B.F.S.P., XVII, 489. See also Doc. No. L in Strupp, *op. cit.*, pp. 107-8.

[17] Article III, Decree of the Fourth National Assembly, July 22 (Aug. 3), 1829, B.F.S.P., XVI, 898. See also note 16, *supra*.

[18] Letter (Particular) of Capodistrias to Leopold, April 6, 1830, Inclosure "B" with Letter of Leopold to the Plenipotentiaries, May 15, 1830, Doc. No. 39, *ibid.*, XVII, 494-96.

[19] Memorandum affirming the Observations of the Senate on the Protocol of Feb. 3, 1830, inclosed with Leopold's Letter to Lord Aberdeen, May 23, 1830, Doc. No. 44, *ibid.*, p. 504.

THE FORFEITURE OF SOVEREIGNTY

the future of the country" and made it impossible for him to fulfill "the engagements contracted with the nation" concerning its definitive form of government.[20]

The protecting powers, however, were determined to exclude from the international agreements which created the Greek monarchy any commitment concerning its constitutional limitation. "In making Greece an independent and monarchical state," ran their reply to the Greek Senate, "the three Courts have abstained from anticipating the nature of the institutions and the laws to be derived from this form of government. They believe that under the auspices of the future sovereign these institutions will be suited to the true interests, the real needs, and the legitimate wishes of Greece and will secure for it a long future of peace, order and happiness."[21] The issue was thus clearly joined. The Government of Greece believed that the monarchy should be limited by a constitution stemming from the constituent assemblies of the Revolution and consented to by ruler and people. The protecting powers, on the other hand, insisted on unconditional acceptance of the monarchy, apparently believing (in the words of Capodistrias paraphrasing Hobbes) that the sovereignty of the nation had become "absorbed and concentrated" in the person of the monarch.

During the period of anarchy and civil war which followed the assassination of Capodistrias, the protecting powers placed Greece under their undisguised tutelage. They advanced the claim that, having contributed decisively to Greek independence as "the only means of establishing durable peace in the Near East," they had "not only the right but the obligation" to intervene in order to pacify the country internally as well.[22] This claim, which would no doubt have been gratefully upheld by a long-suffering people, was amply warranted by the com-

---

[20] Item 4, Annex "A," Report of the Residents of the Three Courts in Greece to the Plenipotentiaries in London, April 19, 1830, Protocol, London, July 1, 1830, Doc. No. 33, *ibid.*, XVIII, 609.
[21] Protocol, London, July 1, 1830, Doc. No. 33, *ibid.*, pp. 605–6.
[22] Protocol, London, March 7, 1832, Doc. No. 42, *ibid.*, XIX, 9–10.

plete breakdown of authority in Greece.[23] The Capodistrians and the constitutionalists had formed rival governments, convoked rival assemblies, and had thus reduced national sovereignty to an abstraction. And since the election of an indisputably representative assembly was impossible under the circumstances,[24] the protecting powers constituted themselves the trustees of national sovereignty pending its transmission to the king whom they undertook to select after the withdrawal of Prince Leopold as a candidate.[25]

That this was the powers' conception of their role was shown by their determination to block any action, until after the King's arrival, on two vital issues—the drafting of a monarchical constitution and the distribution of the national domain. Despite their fierce dissensions, the two rival factions were substantially agreed that the King, before his accession, should enter into a compact with the nation by signifying his adherence to a constitution drafted by a National Assembly. The first attempt to frame such a document was made by the so-called fifth National Convention, which represented the Capodistrian party and was convoked at Argos in December, 1831, by Agostino Capodistrias, the deceased President's brother and would-be successor. The Constitution which was submitted to this assembly in March, 1832, by a drafting committee of considerable intellectual distinction aimed to adapt the political principles of the Revolution—civil liberty, national sovereignty, and representative institutions—to the monarchical form of government.[26] Beginning, as usual, with provisions about the state religion, citizenship, and naturalization, it proceeded to a comprehensive and liberal formulation of the "rights and duties of the Greeks." It declared that the state exercised its authority "through the various agencies of government as the representa-

[23] "A," Confidential Memorandum on the State of Greece by Stratford Canning to Agostino Capodistrias, Dec. 28, 1831, with Protocol, London, March 7, 1832, Doc. No. 42, *ibid.*, pp. 11–13.

[24] *Ibid.*

[25] *Ibid.*, pp. 9–10.

[26] Alex. P. Couclelis, *Les Régimes gouvernementaux de la Grèce de 1821 à nos jours*, pp. 25–26.

tive of the nation"; and it defined the Greek State as a "hereditary, constitutional, and parliamentary monarchy." It vested the legislative power "jointly in the King, the Senate and the House of Representatives," and the executive power in the "hereditary Chief of the nation," to be exercised through ministers appointed by him, but responsible to the legislature. It provided a five-year term for the lower house, indirect election with progressively steep property qualifications, and annual renewal of its membership by one fifth. It conferred on the Crown the right to appoint the members of the Senate for life, to dissolve the House of Representatives subject to reconvocation of its successor within three months, and to exercise a suspensive veto over measures originating with either branch of the legislature. It provided for a procedure of consultation between the executive and the legislature as well as between the upper and the lower branch of the latter, gave to both the right to amend or to reject government measures, but authorized their reintroduction in the following session. Finally, while it conferred parity on the two houses in all other respects, it confined legislative initiative on financial and economic measures to the House of Representatives.[27]

This Constitution, whose completion synchronized with the designation of Prince Otho of Bavaria as king of Greece, was stillborn. The Assembly accepted it as the "fundamental law of the nation," instructed the Government to submit it to the King, and authorized the legislature to amend it in accordance with his "observations" in order to secure royal assent to its promulgation.[28] But before these instructions could be carried out, the Government of Agostino Capodistrias collapsed and was succeeded by an unstable coalition in which the constitutionalists became increasingly dominant.

The fourth National Convention (which was reconvoked by the new Government with a view to emphasizing the illegality

[27] *Ibid.*, p. 25. Details are given by Aravantinos in *Constitutional Law of Greece*, p. 333n.

[28] *Ibid.*, p. 26. Footnote 1 states that action of the Assembly is given by Aravantinos, *op. cit.*, p. 355n.

of its immediate predecessor) unanimously ratified Prince Otho's selection and proceeded to take action on the distribution of the national domain and on the Constitution. But its deliberations were halted by a note from the three powers, which denied the Assembly's competence to "draft or even to discuss a constitution" or any other fundamental law "without the coöperation of the monarch," and contended that such action "would be at variance with the Greek people's mandate to the three Courts" to designate the King of Greece.[29] While a minority of experienced members advocated a more positive recognition of "the right of the Crown to participate in legislation and even in the framing of the constitution," the majority upheld the Assembly's initiative with respect to the latter function. Its reply to the powers' note called attention to the fact that "even President Capodistrias had invariably recognized the Assembly's right to the sovereign power," admitted that the establishment of the monarchy had modified this power "with respect to fundamental laws" and that the constitution was therefore subject to revision by the King or the Regency "after their arrival in Greece," but insisted that the initial drafting of the constitution was the duty of the representatives of the Greek people.[30]

This protest was the swansong of the constitutionalism which had been dominant during the Insurrection. The Assembly which so proudly pitted its sovereign power against the will of the European Concert was soon afterward dispersed by the unruly Rumeliot soldiery. The passing of the last elected body of the Revolution symbolized the transfer of sovereignty from the nation to the monarch. In default of a constitution drawn up by the representatives of the people and conferring certain powers on the Crown as one of the several organs of the state, it was now left to the initiative of the Crown to decide whether

[29] Decree of Fourth National Assembly, Pronia, Aug. 8, 1832, B.F.S.P., XIX, 1251. See also Couclelis, *op. cit.*, p. 27. Footnote 3 states that the text of the Residents' reply to the Fourth National Assembly, Aug. 10, 1832, is given by Aravantinos, *op. cit.*, p. 344n.

[30] Couclelis, *op. cit.*, pp. 27–28. Details are given by Aravantinos, *op. cit.*, p. 344n.

and to what extent the nation would be admitted to a share in its own governance. This transfer had already been formally registered in an international transaction. By the Treaty of May 7, 1832, "the hereditary sovereignty of Greece" was offered "by the Courts of France, Great Britain, and Russia, duly authorized thereto by the Greek nation," to Prince Otho with the title "King of Greece," and was accepted on his behalf (owing to his minority) by his father, the King of Bavaria. Greece, "under the sovereignty of Prince Otho and the guarantee of the three Courts," was erected into a "monarchical, independent State"; and it was stipulated that pending the King's majority, "his rights of sovereignty" would be exercised "in their entire plenitude" by a regency of three members appointed by the King of Bavaria.[31]

The Treaty of May 7, 1832, was negotiated and signed by the British, French and Russian Governments "exercising the power to choose a sovereign for Greece bestowed on them by the Greek people."[32] Completely ignoring the pronouncements of successive national assemblies, the three Governments assumed that this power was "unconditional" and that it implied *a priori* acceptance of their candidate by his future subjects. They read into their mandate more "implied powers" when they agreed, on behalf of Greece, to provisions regulating the succession and the King's majority, authorizing the King of Bavaria to establish a regency, and making detailed stipulations about a loan to be contracted by "Prince Otho of Bavaria, as King of Greece, under the guarantee of the three powers."[33] The implications of this transaction were prejudicial to the fiscal independence of Greece. For the treaty further provided that interest and amortization charges should have first lien on the receipts of the Greek treasury, gave the diplomatic representatives of the three powers the right to supervise the execution of this stipulation, and earmarked the proceeds of the loan for possible com-

---

[31] (A)—Convention Relative to the Sovereignty of Greece between the Three Allied Courts and Bavaria, London, May 7, 1832, with Protocol, London, May 7, 1832, Doc. No. 45, B.F.S.P., XIX, 33–41.
[32] *Ibid.*, p. 33.   [33] Articles X and XII, *ibid.*, pp. 37–39.

pensation to the Ottoman Government in return for a more favorable territorial settlement.[34] Finally, the treaty invaded the domain of national defense by authorizing the recruiting of a Bavarian corps of 3,500, "equipped and paid by the Greek State," to replace the troops of the three powers stationed in Greece.[35] Thus, owing partly to the anarchy that beset Greece eleven years after the outbreak of the Insurrection and partly no doubt to the eagerness of the three Courts to choose the easiest and the most congenial way of settling the Greek question, the mandate to select a king ultimately led to the alienation of Greek sovereignty. Greece was declared independent of the Ottoman Empire, but was placed under the tutelage of the protecting powers who in turn, by the Treaty of May 7, 1832, transferred their charge to the King of Bavaria and through him to the Regency and to King Otho. For all her "independence," Greece thus became both externally and internally a Bavarian protectorate[36] under the suzerain control implicit in the ambiguous "guarantee" of the three powers.

III

The first consequence of this alienation of sovereignty for the internal governance of Greece was the transfer of the constituent power from the nation to the monarch. What use would he make of it? The unrepresentative and impotent assemblies of the post-Capodistrian period had failed to reduce the Crown to the status of one of the organs of the State through a constitution of popular origin. Could the Greek people now expect at least an instrument similar to the French Charter of 1814 registering a voluntary grant of power by the Crown to the nation? Though the constitutional question was broached in the course of the negotiations, the Treaty of May 7, 1832, was silent on the self-limitation of the monarchy. On the other hand, the proclamation of August 30, 1832, issued by the London Confer-

---

[34] Article XIII, *ibid.*, p. 39.
[35] Article XIV, *ibid.*, p. 39.
[36] Articles XV, XVI, and XVII, *ibid.*, p. 40. See also Treaty between Bavaria and Greece, Nov. 1, 1832, *ibid.*, XX, 733.

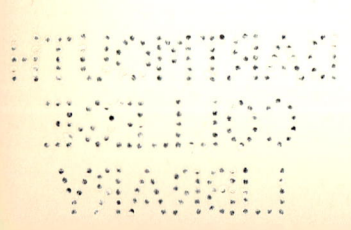

ence on the completion of its labors, called upon the Greek people to "rally round the throne" and to "assist their King in the task of giving the State a definitive constitution."[37] The implication of this appeal was in agreement with the more explicit promise given by the Bavarian Government. Its note of July 31, 1832, addressed by M. de Gise, the Foreign Minister, to S. Tricoupis, Greek Secretary of State, began with a firm rejection of the Greek people's claim to the constituent power. It asserted that the exercise of this power would violate the Greek mandate to the three Courts, since it contained "no mention of a definitive constitution of the state drawn up before the election of the monarch and without his assistance." After thus affirming the sovereignty of the Crown, however, the Bavarian note concluded with the declaration that one of the first matters to claim the attention of the Regency would be the convocation of a "general assembly of the nation" to collaborate in drawing up a definitive constitution.[38]

The Regency not only failed to redeem this pledge, but it gave short shrift to the suggestion of several constitutionalist leaders that it call a national assembly for a short session in order to receive from it a mandate to govern similar to those repeatedly given to President Capodistrias.[39] "The Regency," wrote approvingly Prokesh-Osten, the Austrian Minister in Athens, "made its début with a measure that was both necessary and correct by rejecting the claim that the sovereignty of the people is the source of royal authority." And if there were still any doubts left on this score, they were dispelled by the first royal proclamation in which "Otho, by the grace of God King of Greece," pledged himself to protect the religion of the coun-

[37] Declaration [of the Allied Courts] to the Greeks, Aug. 30, 1832, *ibid.*, XIX, 1253–54. Annex "D," Protocol, London, April 26, 1832. Doc. No. 44, *ibid.*, XIX, 25–26.

[38] Finlay, *op. cit.*, VII, 115. Note 2 states that the letter of Baron de Gise, dated 31st July, 1832, is printed in *Recueil des traités, actes et pièces concernants la fondation de la royauté en Grèce et le tracé de ses limites* (Nauplie, 1833), p. 62. An excerpt is quoted by Driault, *Histoire diplomatique de la Grèce de 1821 à nos jours*, II, 86–87. See also Aravantinos, *op. cit.*, p. 356, note 62, as cited by Couclelis, *op. cit.*, p. 29.

[39] Driault, *op cit.*, II, 129–31; 137; see also p. 72, *supra*.

try, to uphold the laws, and to "preserve inviolable . . . the independence, the liberties, and the rights of the Greek people,"[40] but sedulously avoided any commitment on the constitutional issue. It was apparently settled that the sovereignty of the Greek people was henceforth to be vested in the monarchy which seemed determined to remain unfettered whether by restrictions of popular origin or by self-imposed limitations.

The primary aim of the Greek Insurrection—the overthrow of Ottoman rule—was attained after nearly ten years of bitter war against the Sultan and his Egyptian vassal, and thanks largely to the armed intervention of the three most powerful European Governments. They made it unmistakably clear that they intended the independence of Greece from the Ottoman Empire to be genuine and complete when they rejected the Turkish Government's request for (a) the limitation of the Greek army and navy to the minimum necessary to internal order, (b) a pledge of perpetual neutrality on the part of Greece and her citizens in all future wars against Turkey, and (c) the surrender of Turkish subjects who had participated in the Insurrection and after the end of hostilities had taken refuge in Greece. In reply to these demands the three powers pointed out that the maintenance of armed forces free from foreign control and participation in any war breaking out between third parties are rights "inherent in the independence of a state" unless it has been "constituted and declared perpetually neutral"; that the independence of Greece "and all the rights inherent therein" had been recognized by the London Protocol of February 3, 1830, to which the Ottoman Government had fully acceded; and that the surrender of political refugees was a matter of domestic concern on which they would not presume to dictate to the Government of independent Greece.[41] This frustration of the last Turkish attempt to limit Greek sovereignty justified the Duke of Broglie's triumphant declaration: "Greece exists, she is independent, all Europe recognizes

[40] Excerpt from Otho's Proclamation, June 1, 1835, Driault, *op. cit.*, II, 137.
[41] Item 20, Protocol of the Three Protecting Powers, London, Aug. 30, 1832, Doc. No. 52, B.F.S.P., XXII, 933.

her."[42] But this goal had been reached at considerable cost. Neither the strains and stresses of war nor the intervention of the essentially anti-revolutionary and monarchical European powers were favorable to the development of constitutionalism, republicanism, and democracy in insurgent Greece. It was therefore inevitable that the military and diplomatic success of the Insurrection should have been purchased with defeat on the domestic front; and that both the independence and the internal sovereignty of the new state should be tempered by the "guarantee" of the protecting powers with all its vague implications. Yet to a people weary with war and civil strife—indeed to contemporary European and world opinion—deliverance from Ottoman rule was so brilliant an achievement that it was gratefully accepted, even though it was not accompanied by complete national self-determination or by internal self-government.

[42] Address of the Duke of Broglie in the French Senate regarding the affairs of Greece, May 18, 1833, Doc. No. LXIV, Strupp, *op. cit.,* p. 155.

Chapter Five

THE LIMITED MONARCHY OF OTHO

I

THE COMPROMISE described in the last chapter—the impairment of sovereignty and the surrender of self-government in exchange for complete independence from Ottoman rule—did not prove permanent. Its revision during the next hundred years was incidental to the successive and more-or-less-violent shifts of political power which have punctuated the history of modern Greece. A full discussion of these periodic crises, which were, as usual, due to international as well as to domestic factors, would be outside the scope of this study. What will concern us in the following three chapters is merely the part played in them by each of the three participants in the constitutional settlement of 1830–32, namely, the protecting powers, the monarchy, and the Greek nation.

The first of these crises was essentially a revolt of the disaffected politicians who represented the ruling oligarchy of the War of Independence against King Otho's system of autocratic government by Bavarian bureaucrats. It originated in the *coup d'état* of September, 1843, which enabled the leaders of the revolt, effectively supported by the Athens garrison, to supplant the hereditary ruler as the source of authority in the state and to take a series of steps designed to convert the Othonian regime of monarchical absolutism into a limited monarchy. This revolutionary change was effected, in the name of the sovereign people, by the Council of State—King Otho's solitary and grudging concession to constitutionalism during the first part of his reign.[1] "Compelled by the irresistible force of circumstances to assume extraordinary powers," this body prescribed a new oath

---

[1] Letter of M. A. Metaxas, President of Council of Ministers to Sir Edmund Lyons, Sept. 16, 1843, Inclosure 2 with Letter of Lyons to Lord Aberdeen, Sept.

for the armed forces of the state, which transferred their allegiance "to the constitutional throne and the constitutional institutions to be created by the National Assembly"; and having thus anticipated the course of events, it demanded "immediate and full acceptance" by the King of an implementary program which included principally: (*a*) the formation of a new ministry under A. Metaxas, the chief of the "Russian" party and the political leader of the insurrection, and (*b*) the convocation within a month of a National Assembly "to deliberate and to decide, in agreement with the Crown, concerning a definitive constitution."[2]

In so far as King Otho's acquiescence in these revolutionary proceedings implied recognition of a higher authority than his own, he had sufficient reason to complain to the envoys of the protecting powers that he had "abdicated his royal prerogatives and was no longer King."[3] At the same time, while his "personal inclinations were unavoidably coerced,"[4] and the royal signature affixed to the decree which convoked the National Assembly symbolized the surrender of sovereignty, the terms of the same decree, by stipulating that the Assembly would collaborate with the King in framing a constitution, secured for the Crown a share in the exercise of the constituent power.[5]

As a matter of fact, the Constitution of 1844 was for the most part the work of a National Assembly dominated by the constitutionalists, who had been in eclipse since the Capodistrian dictatorship, under the leadership of the veteran Alexander Mavrocordatos.[6] It was originally drafted by a committee of twenty-one, of which Mavrocordatos and S. Tricoupis, the lead-

---

17, 1843, Doc. No. 2, Great Britain, Foreign Office, *British and Foreign State Papers*, XXX, 942. See also *The Cambridge History of British Foreign Policy*, edited by Ward and Gooch, II, 592–93.

[2] Address of Council of State to King Otho, Sept. 15, 1843, Inclosure 4 with Letter of Lyons to Aberdeen, Sept. 17, 1843, Doc. No. 2, B.F.S.P., XXXII, 943.

[3] Driault, *Histoire diplomatique de la Grèce* . . ., II, 240.

[4] Letter from Aberdeen to Lyons, Oct. 25, 1843, Doc. No. 5, B.F.S.P., XXXII, 947.

[5] Ordinance convoking a National Assembly, Athens, Sept. 15, 1843, Inclosure 5 with Doc. No. 2, Letter of Lyons to Aberdeen, Sept. 17, 1843, *ibid.*, p. 944.

[6] Letter of Lyons to Aberdeen, Oct. 10, 1843, Doc. No. 6, *ibid.*, p. 949. See also Finlay, *A History of Greece* . . ., VII, 180.

ers of the "English" party, John Kolettes, the leader of the "French" party, and D. Kyriakós, the foremost constitutional lawyer of the Assembly, were the most prominent members; and having been debated and revised by the Assembly, it was submitted by the drafting committee to the King, who was invited to make such "observations" as he "might deem necessary."[7] A comparison of these observations with the draft of the Assembly and the definitive text of the constitution shows that the King made a determined, and not wholly unsuccessful, effort to retain the major part of his power under the forms of constitutional government.

With a view to avoiding the "false interpretation" that the rights of the Crown were limited by the articles which defined the King's authority, he proposed that the executive power should be described as belonging to the King "who exercises it through responsible ministers appointed by him." But the Assembly insisted on its own version, which named the King as the source of the executive power, but entrusted its exercise to "responsible ministers," thus giving them independent constitutional status and raising them above the level of mere executive agents of the Crown. Similarly, the Assembly refused to make the Crown the "source of the judicial power." It retained its original draft which declared that "the judicial power is exercised by the Courts," but inserted in another place the innocuous statement that the King is the "source of justice." Further, while the King desired to confine ministerial countersignature only to those of his acts which "pertained to the public service," the Assembly disallowed this qualification. It also rejected the King's suggestion that the safeguard of ministerial countersignature be dispensed with in the case of a change of ministry and wrote into the constitution the provision that all the decrees relative thereto must be countersigned by the incoming premier after he has been nominated and sworn in.[8]

[7] Address of the Deputation of the National Assembly charged to lay before the King the Project of the Constitution, Inclosure 4 with Letter of Lyons to Aberdeen, March 21, 1844, Doc. No. 29, B.F.S.P., XXXII, 979.

[8] Note addressed by King Otho to the National Assembly, Feb. 28, 1844, In-

As regards the treaty-making power, the King and the Assembly distinguished between treaties of peace and alliance, which it was agreed should be concluded by the executive and communicated to Parliament only in case the interests of the state permitted publication, and commercial treaties which required legislative implementation or imposed individual burdens on citizens, and for which the consent of the Chamber of Deputies and the Senate was stipulated. With respect to the power of appointment, however, there was serious and significant disagreement. The King proposed the excision of the provision forbidding nomination by the executive to an office not previously created by law. He contended that this prohibition might prevent the Government from meeting unforeseen administrative needs, and he argued that the limitation inherent in budgetary appropriations would be a sufficient safeguard against possible abuse of the appointive power. But the Assembly remained obdurate and retained the restrictive clause. On the other hand, it accepted several amendments to the articles which dealt with the King's relations with Parliament. It conceded to him the right to convoke the chambers in extraordinary session at his discretion and in ordinary session once a year, and the right of dissolution followed by new elections within two months and convocation of the new chambers within three. It also expanded, at the King's suggestion, the royal right to pardon, so as to include the right to grant an amnesty "on the responsibility of the entire ministry." And though it had originally fixed the Civil List for the duration of the reign, it accepted the King's request for a more flexible arrangement designed to "ensure the independence of the Crown," and made ten years its minimum duration. At the same time, certain proposed modifications of the royal oath which reflected a rather exalted "divine right" view of the monarch's station were rejected by the Assembly; and so was the request for the excision of the article which provided for a temporary regency by the

---

closure 5 with Letter of Lyons to Aberdeen, March 21, 1844, Doc. No. 29, *ibid.*, pp. 980 ff.

ministry in the event of the King's death during his minority, or the absence of a successor, and pending the swearing-in of the lawful regent.[9]

More significant was the King's attempt to limit by constitutional provision the membership of the elective Chamber of Deputies, and at the same time to remove all restrictions to his right to nominate members of the Senate and to dispense with the ministerial countersignature of all appointments to that body. The Assembly fixed the minimum membership of the lower and of the upper house at eighty and twenty-seven, respectively; and while it limited the King's power to appoint senators to a maximum of one-half the members of the lower house, it left the size of the latter to be determined "in proportion to population," by legislative enactment. On the other hand, it accepted the King's proposal to confine the countersigning of senatorial appointments to the Prime Minister with the proviso that his signature would be construed to express concurrence of the entire ministry. Furthermore, at the King's request the Assembly extended the privilege of appointment for life to those members of the Court of Accounts who sat in a deliberative capacity, but, contrary to the King's suggestion, it withheld life tenure from justices of the peace. Despite the King's cogent representations, it also remained adamant on the repeal of laws and decrees contrary to the constitution and on the exclusion of non-citizens from public office—a provision which did violence to King Otho's Panhellenic nationalism.[10]

The Constitution of 1844 can thus be called a negotiated instrument—"a compact between King and nation"—since it was produced by the concurrent exercise of the constituent power and it was signed and promulgated by the King.[11] At the same time, the fact that it was initiated by an Assembly of

---

[9] Note of the Assembly on King Otho's Observations (Art. XXIII *et al.*), Inclosure 6 with Letter of Lyons to Aberdeen, March 21, 1844, Doc. No. 29, *ibid.*, pp. 987–88.

[10] Articles III and CIII, Constitution of 1844, *ibid.*, p. 988.

[11] Letter of Lyons to Aberdeen, Dec. 21, 1843, Doc. No. 18, *ibid.*, pp. 960–61. See also Proclamation announcing King Otho's acceptance of the Constitution,

revolutionary origin and that it was practically imposed upon a reluctant monarch, would seem to make it also an expression of the general will, the product of popular sovereignty.[12] But whatever the "literary theory" as to the origins of the Constitution of 1844, the fact remains that within its framework the monarchy retained the major part of its authority. In the first place, the silence of the Constitution on the question of the source of sovereignty amounted to acceptance of the orthodox view of limited monarchy, according to which the monarch, notwithstanding the constitutional restraints on his authority, remains sovereign and, hence, retains all the powers he has not explicitly yielded and can do everything that the Constitution does not expressly forbid. Moreover, the King's participation in the framing of the Constitution established his claim to a share of the constituent power and made his consent a prerequisite to revision. At the same time, the extensive powers he retained, which included an absolute legislative veto, the right to appoint and to dismiss his ministers, to nominate the members of the Senate for life, to dissolve the Chamber of Deputies, and to issue executive decrees, secured for him a predominant position over all other organs of the State.[13] In short, the regime established by the Greek Constitution of 1844 was, both in its constitutional and in its broader political aspects, very similar to that of the July Monarchy in France. In both, the existing political order, which was based on the principles of legitimacy and monarchical sovereignty, was overthrown by insurrection. The outcome was in both cases a quasi-legitimate regime of limited monarchy; and the limitation was effected by means of a Constitution which, though dictated (by a parliamentary caucus in France and by a National Assembly in Greece), was euphemistically called a compact between

---

March 16, 1844, Inclosure 11 with Letter of Lyons to Aberdeen, March 21, 1844, Doc. No. 29, *ibid.*, pp. 1000–1001.

[12] Constitution as voted by the National Assembly and accepted by King Otho, March 16, 1844, Inclosure 10 with Letter of Lyons to Aberdeen, March 21, 1844, Doc. No. 29, *ibid.*, pp. 989–1000.

[13] *Ibid.*

the monarch and the nation. Like the revised Charter of 1830, the Greek Constitution of 1844 conferred on the Crown extensive powers quite at variance with the principle that "the King reigns, but does not rule," which presumably summed up the political philosophy of its French prototype. Finally, in both countries these powers were further expanded by the manner in which the monarchs interpreted their respective constitutions and conducted their governments. And since no provision was made for an amending process and since neither Louis Philippe nor Otho would take the initiative of orderly constitutional revision, the two regimes were eventually brought to an end extra-legally, by the higher power to which they owed their existence—the general will expressing itself through insurrection.[14]

II

The attitude of the protecting powers toward the insurrection of 1843 and the ensuing constitutional settlement should have been determined by what they conceived to be their obligations as signatories and "guarantors" of the Treaty of May 7, 1832, which placed the Bavarian dynasty on the throne of Greece. But these legal obligations were tempered—in fact dominated—by the exigencies of political interest. Greece was a small and weak state, in the founding of which the Concert of Europe had played a decisive part. To a greater extent than any other independent country, she was dependent on the good will of the great powers, and her domestic politics were largely dominated by their rivalries. She therefore provided a peculiarly propitious stage for that ideological sham battle of liberalism and constitutionalism against absolutism, which anticipated by exactly one hundred years the analogous international conflict between democracy and fascism, as a convenient disguise for the struggle for power among the major European

[14] Letter of Mr. P. C. Scarlett, British Minister at Athens, to Lord Russell, Oct. 24, 1862, Doc. No. 7, *ibid.*, LVIII, 1014–17, and Letter of Russell to Scarlett, Nov. 6, 1862, Doc. No. 20, *ibid.*, pp. 1027–28. Russell's letter also Doc. LXVI in Strupp, *La Situation internationale de la Grèce*, pp. 162–63.

states. Though their policy on the constitutional issue in Greece was considerably influenced by the personal vicissitudes of Greek politics, it may be said that on the whole, Great Britain and France, the two liberal powers, had been fairly consistent in urging King Otho to grant a constitution. "The habits and genius and geographical distribution of the nation," wrote Palmerston in 1835 to Sir Edmund Lyons, the British Minister in Athens, "their ancient history and recent struggle; their national assemblies during the War of Independence; the expectations they have been encouraged to form—all these things combine to make it impossible that they can be contented to go on under an absolute monarchy."[15] At the other extreme stood Prokesh-Osten, the Austrian Minister in Athens, who did not represent one of the protecting powers yet who exerted greater personal influence over King Otho than did any of his colleagues. Though opposed to constitutionalism, as befitted a diplomatic agent of Metternich, he was less concerned with doctrines than with the King's interests, and therefore ended by advising him to accede to the wishes of the nation in order to enhance his popularity and consolidate the position of his house.[16] Finally, Russia, the third of the protecting powers, while inclined to look favorably on Otho's absolutism, was antagonized by his eccelesiastical policy. The Erastian Decree of 1833—a virtual Act of Supremacy which severed all connection with the Patriarchate of Constantinople and subjected the Church of Greece to a Catholic monarch—was not calculated to strengthen Russian sympathy for the Bavarian dynasty; and the situation was exacerbated by the steadfast refusal of King Otho and of his brother and heir Luitpold to follow an illustrious precedent and declare the Greek throne well worth a Mass. That the *coup d'état* of September, 1843, was encouraged, if not inspired, by Russian hostility to Otho, is evidenced by the fact that its chief promoter was, as we have seen, the leader of

[15] *The Cambridge History of British Foreign Policy*, II, 589, quoted from Sir S. M. Eardley-Wilmot, *Life of Vice-Admiral Lord Lyons*, pp. 77 ff. Cf. Finlay, *A History of Greece*, VII, 299.
[16] Driault, *op. cit.*, II, 240.

the "Russian" party. But Russian hostility could have been more than checkmated by British and French support. As a matter of fact, the insurrection was immediately endorsed by the other two protecting powers, because, apart from their theoretical aversion to Otho's absolutism and their desire to have in Greece a regime created in their own image, they expected the constitutional ministries to show greater solicitude than King Otho for the bondholders of the loan contracted under Article XII of the Treaty of May 7, 1832, and for British and French interests generally.[17]

It would appear then that from the standpoint of political interest the protecting powers were far from hostile to the change initiated by the *coup d'état* of September, 1843. What was their legal position as signatories and "guarantors" of the treaties which had created the Kingdom of Greece? These treaties decreed that the government of Greece should be a monarchy, but did not stipulate that it should not be constitutional. Hence, even if they had not condoned—or abetted—the Insurrection, the protecting powers could justifiably claim that its ultimate outcome—the constitutional settlement of 1844—did not violate the international agreements which recognized the independence of Greece and conferred upon her a monarchical form of government.

This was the position taken by the British and French Governments. The first dispatch which Lord Aberdeen, the British Foreign Secretary, sent to Sir Edmund Lyons after receiving the news of the *coup d'état,* while mildly deprecating "the forcible mode by which the change was effected," praised the Greek people for having conducted themselves in a manner "so different from the example afforded by countries more advanced in civilization." His Lordship then proceeded to define the role of the three "guarantor" powers. "It may be necessary," he wrote, that they should "exert themselves to moderate the projects of the Greek patriots; since . . . it is by no means impos-

---

[17] Letter of Aberdeen to Lyons, Oct. 25, 1843, Doc. No. 5, B.F.S.P., XXXII, 947. See also Article XII, Treaty of May 7, 1832, *ibid.,* XIX, 38–39.

sible that crude, exaggerated, and impracticable propositions may be brought forward at the meeting of the National Assembly. . . . But it will also be our duty to impress upon the King the wisdom, and indeed the necessity, of strictly adhering to his promises and of religiously fulfilling the pledges which he has given to his people."[18] Acceptance of the *fait accompli,* coupled with counsels of moderation to the Assembly and of constitutional behavior to the King—such was the British Foreign Secretary's interpretation of the powers' duty under the "guarantee" in relation to the crisis of 1843. The Greek people's right to insurrection was not denied; but at the same time the protecting powers' right to intervention was unequivocally affirmed.

The form which this intervention should take was elaborately prescribed in a subsequent dispatch from the same quarter. Lord Aberdeen began by announcing a serious rift in the Concert of the three powers. "Although," he wrote, "a difference of opinion may exist between the Courts of Great Britain and France and that of Russia on the constitutional question . . . we anticipate no opposition on the part of Russia to the proceedings of the Greek Government and the National Assembly." He was able to give similar reassurance concerning the attitude of the fourth signatory of the Treaty of May 7, 1832—the King of Bavaria. But this promise of non-interference was accompanied by His Majesty's urgent recommendation "that the royal authority should be fixed on a broad and solid basis and that such checks should be placed on the tendency to undue extension of the democratic principle as shall prevent any encroachment on the just power of the throne." The British Foreign Secretary proceeded, with obvious relish, to expand this text into a sermon on constitutional orthodoxy with the concurrence of the French Ambassador in London, though not of his Russian colleague, who had been "precluded from taking any part in such questions." He expressed, it is true, some qualms about the propriety of foreign powers appearing to impose

[18] *Ibid.,* XXXII, 947–48.

upon the King and the people of Greece "a constitution ready prepared for their acceptance"; but he hastened to silence these misgivings with the reflection that it was after all "incumbent on the protecting powers to watch over the progress and completion of that constitution which, by their repeated declarations, the Greek people have been led to expect at their hands." Thus reassured, His Lordship "recommended," on behalf of the British and French Governments, that the following principles should be incorporated in the constitution:

the inviolability of the King; the nomination by the royal authority to all offices, both civil and military; the exercise by the Crown of equal power in making laws with the other branches of the legislature; the existence of two Chambers, one elective, the other, of which the members should be hereditary or for life, to be nominated by the King. The right of the Crown to summon or to dissolve the Chambers, subject to the control possessed by them, from the necessity of their concurrence in the estimates and votes of supply for the public service.

After adding to this list that the legislature should meet annually, and that all money bills should originate exclusively with the Crown, Lord Aberdeen instructed Sir Edmund to discountenance "wild theories or extravagant notions respecting the extension of the democratic franchise," to point out the dangers of a unicameral legislature, and to suggest the advisability of an elective franchise "widely extended" yet "founded on a representation of property." The note concluded with the timely advice to confine the franchise to Greek citizens, for "its extension to subjects of the Porte would afford just cause of umbrage to the Turkish Government."[19]

The principles laid down in this revealing document are precisely those on which the constitutional settlement of the insurrection of 1843 was founded. In view of the fact that the most influential members of the Assembly and of the drafting committee were the leaders of the "English" party,[20] that they

---

[19] Letter of Aberdeen to Lyons, Nov. 25, 1843, Doc. No. 8, *ibid.*, pp. 950–54.
[20] Letter of Lyons to Aberdeen, Dec. 6, 1843, Doc. No. 16, *ibid.*, p. 959.

were in constant consultation with the British Minister, and that the latter followed the constitutional debates with extraordinary diligence and discussed them in frequent exchanges with his Chief,[21] the conclusion is warranted that, while the Constitution of 1844 was drafted by the Assembly and slightly amended by the King, its ultimate source of inspiration was the conservative constitutionalism of the British Foreign Secretary. "We desire," said His Lordship, "to establish no British influence, and we equally deprecate the establishment of any other exclusive national influence in Greece."[22] Despite this disclaimer, it was Great Britain—and to a lesser extent the France of Louis Philippe and Guizot—that exploited politically the insurrection of 1843, whatever may have been their responsibility for its outbreak. Lord Aberdeen must have been deeply gratified. For in his final dispatch he dropped for once his customary tone of stern didacticism, commended the "admirable temper" displayed in Greece throughout the crisis, and concluded with the fulsome comment that "such self-command in a popular Assembly convoked under very exciting and critical circumstances is highly creditable to the Greek nation."[23] The Russian Emperor, on the other hand, was correspondingly disappointed by the turn of events in Greece; and he signified his displeasure by recalling his Minister in Athens who had allowed himself to be outgeneraled by his British and French colleagues.[24]

But the recognition of the Greek people's right to change its form of government even by recourse to insurrection did not exhaust the international implications of this change. The part of the Constitution of 1844 which dealt with the regency and the succession, while on the whole patterned after the cognate provisions of the Treaty of May 7, 1832, deviated from them in

---

[21] *Ibid.,* pp. 947–1003 *passim.*
[22] Letter of Aberdeen to Lyons, Nov. 25, 1843, Doc. No. 8, *ibid.,* p. 953.
[23] Letter of Aberdeen to Lyons, April 11, 1844, Doc. No. 31, *ibid.,* p. 1002.
[24] Letter of Lyons to Aberdeen, March 30, 1844: "The Diplomatic Body was invited to the ceremony, and all the Missions were present excepting that of Russia." Doc. No. 30, *ibid.,* p. 1002.

one important particular—the stipulation that the heir to the throne must embrace the faith of the Eastern Orthodox Church.[25] This provision, which was inserted in response to all but unanimous national sentiment, raised the question of primacy as between the international agreements to which King Otho owed his throne and the "compact" he subsequently made with the Greek nation. The King of Bavaria was not disposed to ignore the issue. But the half-hearted endorsement of his reiterated protests by the three powers which were the co-signatories of the Treaty of May 7, 1832, and the strength of Greek sentiment on the religious question, convinced him that, whatever the strictly legal merits of his case, continued intransigence would be inexpedient. A family compact, made during King Otho's sojourn in Bavaria in the summer of 1850, transferred the right of succession from Luitpold, who had categorically refused to abjure Catholicism, to his younger brother Adalbert, who promised to comply with Article XL of the Constitution at the time of his accession.[26] The protecting powers followed suit. "With a view to consolidating the order of succession to the throne of Greece placed under their common guarantee," they concluded with the King of Bavaria and the King of Greece the London Treaty of November 20, 1852, the purpose of which was to bring the Treaty of May 7, 1832, into agreement "with the situation established by Article XL of the Hellenic Constitution."[27]

III

But while Greek sovereignty was implicitly recognized through this adjustment of an international treaty to a national constitution, it was treated with scant respect when it clashed with the interests of the protecting powers. Their interference and dictation was in fact intensified after 1844; and in the

---

[25] Article XL., Constitution, voted by the National Assembly and accepted by King Otho, March 16, 1844, *ibid.*, p. 993.

[26] Driault, *op. cit.*, II, 366–67.

[27] Treaty between Great Britain, Bavaria, France, Greece, and Russia, relative to the Succession to the Crown of Greece, London, Nov. 20, 1852, B.F.S.P., XLI, 36–38.

notorious Don Pacifico case, as well as in the Crimean War, it ran the gamut of coercion from financial pressure to naval occupation.[28] Moreover, though the powers accepted the modification by constitutional enactment of Article VIII of the Treaty of May 7, 1832, they insisted on a strict observance of Article XII of the same Treaty. In a long and minatory dispatch, dated October 2, 1845, Lord Aberdeen instructed Sir Edmund Lyons to call the Greek Government's attention "in language which can no longer be misunderstood or set at naught" to the failure of that year's budget to provide for the service of the foreign debt of Greece; and to declare that this omission was a violation of engagements "clearly determined by Article XII of the Convention of May 7, 1832, by virtue of which the Kingdom of Greece was established under the Bavarian dynasty." The British note warned that "in default of ratification of the Convention of September 14, 1843,"[29] Great Britain would insist "as one of the guaranteeing powers, on the strict execution of the engagements which flow from Article XII above mentioned." These "engagements," which, it should be noted, were entered into by the King of Bavaria and the protecting powers, amounted to foreign dictation on financial policy and by implication on such vital matters as foreign policy and national defense. In 1832, as we have seen, the protecting powers rejected Turkey's proposal to limit the armed forces of Greece; and they based this rejection on the principle that the maintenance of an army and navy free from any foreign control is a right "inherent in the independence of a state."[30] Yet this right, which was so stoutly affirmed against Turkey, apparently had no deterrent effect on the protecting powers themselves. "We shall not cease," wrote the British Foreign Secretary, "to urge and require the introduction of a sys-

[28] Correspondence between officials of the Governments of Great Britain and Greece re Don Pacifico's claim on the Greek Government, 1847–49, *ibid.*, XXXIX, 332 ff. Cf. *The Cambridge History of British Foreign Policy*, II, 330–31, 596–99.
[29] Letter of Aberdeen to Lyons, Doc. No. 1, B.F.S.P., XLV, 557.
[30] Protocol of Plenipotentiaries of France, Great Britain, and Russia, London, Aug. 30, 1832, Doc. No. 52, Item 2°, *ibid.*, XXII, 933.

tem of rigid economy in the different branches of the service of the State, and especially in that of the War Department, which is still altogether disproportionate to the real wants of the State . . . and we shall continue to insist on the necessity of administrative reforms and the reduction of the armed forces, as the ministers of the guaranteeing Powers did by the last acts of their Conference in London in 1843." This contrast between the powers' precept to Turkey concerning "the rights inherent in the independence of a state" and their own policy toward Greece strikingly illustrates the ambivalent nature of the sovereignty achieved by that country in 1830 and 1832. Greece was completely independent so far as Turkey was concerned. But the commitments made on her behalf in connection with the loan provided for in Article XII of the Treaty of May 7, 1832, impaired her independence with relation to the "guarantor" powers, the more so because in this instance they seemed to construe their "guarantee" primarily as a safeguard for the bondholders.

Out of respect for the independence of Greece [concluded Lord Aberdeen] Great Britain is unwilling to interfere with her internal affairs. But it is manifest that if Greece desires to be exempt from external control, she must place herself in a position to discharge her own financial obligations without having recourse to the aid of the guaranteeing Powers.[31]

The British Foreign Secretary's warning drove home the lesson that for a weak and easily coercible state, political independence is inseparable from financial solvency; and that when such a state saddles itself with a large foreign debt it renders its sovereignty largely illusory.

[31] Letter of Aberdeen to Lyons, Oct. 2, 1845, Doc. No. 1, *ibid.*, XLV, 558–59.

Chapter Six

THE LIMITED DEMOCRACY OF GEORGE I

I

A FAR MORE DECISIVE test of the policy of the protecting powers and of their obligations under the "guarantee" was presented by the revolt of October, 1862, the dethronement of King Otho, and the expulsion of the Bavarian dynasty. Unlike the *coup d'état* of September, 1843, which was engineered by a handful of politicians and army officers, the insurrection of 1862 reflected a nationwide popular movement.[1] It was presaged by garrison mutinies and street-riots in important provincial centers, and it culminated in an uprising in the capital which was so timed as to synchronize with the King's absence on a protracted tour of the provinces. This uprising was organized by an incongruous combination of veteran politicians, led by the hard-bitten Hydriot oligarch D. Voulgaris, with university students and middle-class intelligentsia, who were inspired by the eloquent young tribune E. Deliyoryis, to emulate the revolutionary role of their peers in Western Europe and especially in nineteenth-century France. The connivance of the army insured the success of the insurrection in Athens; and the end of the Othonian regime was speedily accepted by the country at large because of widespread discontent with the King's internal and foreign policies.

In the field of domestic politics this discontent was due to the fact that King Otho had perverted the Constitution of 1844 into an instrument of monarchical autocracy by a combination of methods which included lavish use of the appointive power,

[1] Letter of Scarlett to Russell, Oct. 24, 1862, Doc. No. 7, Great Britain, Foreign Office, *British and Foreign State Papers*, LXVIII, 1014–17; see also *The Cambridge History of British Foreign Policy*, II, 593, 607.

the building up of a party of King's Friends, managed elections, and extra-parliamentary ministries. It was because John Kolettes was adept at these practices (as well as an exponent of a recklessly nationalistic foreign policy) that he had been during the 1840's the King's favorite Prime Minister in preference to the orthodox constitutionalist Alexander Mavrocordatos. But even the pretense of constitutional and parliamentary government was abandoned after the death of Kolettes and the appointment of such independent political leaders as Mavrocordatos, S. Tricoupis, and A. Metaxas to safely distant legations.[2] Throughout the fifties Greece was governed by a succession of royal ministries headed for the most part by illustrious figureheads. It was the most illustrious of these, the aged Admiral Constantine Kanaris, who attempted, on the eve of the insurrection of 1862, to convert the King to a more constitutional course. When invited to form a government, in January of that year, he outlined his conditions in a comprehensive memorandum which is an accurate picture of the perversion of constitutional government during the latter part of King Otho's reign. The Admiral told the King bluntly that what Greece needed was a complete change of governmental system. To that end he proposed (*a*) that the Crown should confine itself to the nomination of the Prime Minister and allow him to select the rest of the Cabinet in accordance with the balance of power in Parliament; (*b*) that with a view to making the parliamentary situation an approximately accurate reflection of the state of the country, the system of managed elections should be abolished, the King's power to nominate senators should be used more moderately, and the officers of the Royal Household should be excluded from the Senate; (*c*) that (following the precedent established by Sir Robert Peel when he compelled Queen Victoria to part with her Whig ladies-in-waiting) several of these officers should be removed from the King's entourage, presumably because they encouraged him to persist in his un-

[2] *Ibid.*, p. 601. Driault, *Histoire diplomatique de la Grèce de 1821 à nos jours*, II, 133–34, and Finlay, *A History of Greece*, VII, 206–56.

constitutional course; (*d*) that the "Palace Camarilla," which was virtually a super-government and was regarded by public opinion as a "barrier between the people and their King," should be suppressed; and (*e*) that the Crown should conform to the implications of the constitutional doctrine that the king can do no wrong, leave the tasks of government to responsible ministries, and thus arrest the attrition which its authority had suffered as a result of too active participation in politics.[3] When King Otho, having accepted these conditions and nominated Admiral Kanaris to the premiership, compelled him to resign shortly afterward by expressing disapproval of several of the new ministers, he demonstrated for the last time his inability to act as a constitutional monarch; and before the end of the same year he had ceased to be King of Greece.

The decree issued on October 23, 1862, by the leaders of the insurrection (*a*) abolished "the royal rule of Otho and the regency of [Queen] Amalia by unanimous decision of the Greek nation," (*b*) convoked a National Assembly for the purpose of framing a new constitution and electing a new king, and (*c*) set up a triumvirate consisting of D. Voulgaris, president, C. Kanaris, and A. Rouphos, to govern the country provisionally pending the meeting of the Assembly.[4] The first article of this decree terminated the dynastic *status quo* established by the Treaty of May 7, 1832. Yet the protecting powers —the signatories of that treaty and presumably the "guarantors" of its dynastic arrangements—not only refrained from protesting against its unilateral abrogation but also took positive steps calculated to ensure the success of the uprising. The British, French, and Russian Ministers, acting apparently on their own initiative, decided to impress on the King the futility of resistance; and their action was tacitly endorsed by their respective Governments.[5] This unseemly haste, which under the cir-

---

[3] *Ibid.*, pp. 256–58.
[4] Proclamation of the Provisional Government at Athens, Oct. 23, 1862, Inclosure 1 with Letter of Scarlett to Russell, Oct. 24, 1862, Doc. No. 7, B.F.S.P., LVIII, 1017–18.
[5] Letter from Scarlett to Russell, Oct. 24, 1862, Doc. No. 7, *ibid.*, pp. 1014–17.

cumstances amounted to connivance with a violent challenge to established authority, was not motivated by any partiality of the protecting powers for the doctrines of revolution, self-determination, and popular sovereignty. Though their temper had undergone considerable change since they prescribed a monarchical system for Greece, the British, French, and Russian governments still abhorred democratic revolutions, believed in the monarchical form of government and paid lip service to the sanctity of treaties; and they could have invoked these principles and saved King Otho, despite his many and grievous constitutional sins, if they had considered his dethronement prejudicial to their interests. But they took no such view of the situation; and the uprising of October, 1862, achieved its immediate purpose because, in the last analysis, the judgment passed by the Greek people on the Othonian regime substantially agreed with—and was in fact powerfully influenced by—the verdict of the protecting powers.

The attitude of Great Britain, France, and Russia toward the Othonian regime was repeatedly modified during the eventful period which included the revolutionary cycle of 1848, the Crimean War, and the Italian people's successful bid for national unity; but by 1862 it had crystallized into implacable hostility for various and often contradictory reasons. The obvious reluctance of the King's brother and heir to comply with Article XL of the Constitution (which made his conversion to the Eastern Orthodox faith a prerequisite to his accession) created a condition of chronic mistrust on the part of the Russian Government; and the situation was aggravated by recurrent intrigues of the "Russian" party designed to transfer the succession to the Duke of Oldenburg, Queen Amalia's brother and the putative protégé of Russia. Moreover, King Otho's inveterate though largely visionary attachment to the dream of Panhellenic expansion was viewed with deepening suspicion in St. Petersburg, because the Irredentist aspirations of Hellenism were essentially incompatible with the Panslavist movement which became after the Crimean War a decisive factor in Russia's Balkan policies. Napeoleon III, oscillating as usual between revolution and reaction, a revisionist in Italy yet at the same time a defender of the integrity of the Ottoman Empire, distrusted Otho both for his alleged subservience to Austria and as an inveterate instigator of Irredentist insurrection in the Balkan Peninsula.[6] Russian and French hostility, however, might have been neutralized by British friendliness if Otho had been willing to pay the price—a solemn pledge to respect the integrity of the Ottoman Empire, which was the dominant preoccupation of Great Britain's Near Eastern policy. But even the alluring bait of immediate annexation of the Ionian Islands could not induce that romantic monarch to commit Greece to permanent renunciation of the ideal of Panhellenic nationalism. The rejection of this offer, which would have been eagerly seized by a more politic or a less scrupulous ruler, marked Otho definitely in British eyes as a potential disturber of Balkan peace and settled his fate. For it enabled the British Government of that day to adopt toward the King of Greece a policy which was determined by a happy and rare conjunction of interest with principle. The spectacle of one more nation treating its king in accordance with the classic Whig precedent of 1688 was doubly welcome to Lords Palmerston and John Russell—those zealous missionaries of constitutionalism and national self-determination, *in partibus infidelium;* for the victim of the latest emulation of England's example was a monarch at once inveterately unconstitutional and autocratic and singularly unamenable to British dictation in the field of foreign policy.[7] It may be said then that, his constitutional sins apart, King Otho was dethroned because, having incurred the hostility of all three of the protecting powers, whose benevolence was indispensable to Greece, he had come to be regarded by the Greek people as a national liability. By a tragic irony, the most potent cause of this hostility was his passionate attachment

---

[6] Finlay, *A History of Greece*, VII, 250.
[7] Letter of Russell to Scarlett, Nov. 6, 1862, Doc. No. 20, B.F.S.P., LVIII, 1027-28.

to a foreign policy inspired by the "Great Idea," and his determination to identify his reign with the fulfillment of the Greek people's Irredentist aspirations.

II

With this general view of the attitude of the three powers in mind, we must now follow the development of their policy during the crisis precipitated by the Insurrection of October, 1862, in order to determine what they conceived to be their "rights" and "obligations" under the "guarantee" which governed their relations with the Kingdom of Greece. The British Cabinet's first reaction, as interpreted by Lord John Russell, the Foreign Secretary, was unequivocal approval of the insurrection. In his instructions to the British Minister in Athens, he cited the "unsuccessful endeavors" of the British Government to impress upon King Otho the need of careful observance of the constitution, remarked that his "anticipations" as to the consequences of the King's unconstitutional course had been "realized" by the uprising, and formulated a policy of non-intervention in the following terms:

The Kingdom of Greece having by the transactions of 1832 been acknowledged as an independent state, the people of Greece are entitled to exercise the rights of national independence; and one of the rights which belong to an independent nation, and of the exercise of which the history of Europe affords many examples, is that of changing its governing dynasty upon good and sufficient cause.

Since in dethroning King Otho the Greeks had merely exercised this undeniable right, the British Government could see no reason why "any foreign Powers should interfere" in order to compel them "to revoke" their decision.[8]

What then became of Great Britain's "guarantee" of the international agreement which placed King Otho on the throne of Greece? When asked that question by Baron Cetto, the Bavarian Minister in London, His Lordship replied with neat

[8] *Ibid.*

gloss that Article IV of the London Treaty of May 7, 1832, "gave a guarantee to Greece, under the sovereignty of Prince Otho of Bavaria, but no guarantee to King Otho personally." He added that "a guarantee to maintain King Otho on the throne against his own people, and in spite of any faults he might commit," would be "at variance" with the principles of British foreign policy; and that the use of force to restore the deposed ruler was therefore not to be considered. Equally inadmissible would be the "support by force" of the claim of the Bavarian princes to their brother's succession in case he should formally abdicate. For the Treaty of 1852 (which was also invoked by the Bavarian diplomat) "evidently contemplated a peaceable demise of the Crown on the part of King Otho" and presumably laid no obligations on its signatories and guarantors in the event of violent deposition.[9]

But while the British Government recognized in effect that national self-determination included the right to abolish a dynastic *status quo* created by treaty, it was intensely preoccupied with the possible international repercussions of the Greek crisis. It was especially concerned lest the disillusioned and militant nationalism which provided much of the motive force of the insurrection should vent itself in a recrudescence of Irredentist activity directed against the integrity of the Ottoman Empire and the peace of the Near East; and it was equally determined that the change of dynasty in Greece should not redound to the advantage of either of the other two protecting powers. The fear of complications that might arise from Irredentist gestures was easily allayed; for it would have been foolhardy for any Greek Government to ignore Lord Russell's reiterated warning that "no Assembly containing deputies from Turkish provinces would be recognized by Her Majesty as lawfully representing the Kingdom of Greece."[10] But the British Government's efforts to safeguard its position of virtual primacy in Greece were re-

[9] Letter of Russell to Lord Cowley, British Ambassador in Paris, Nov. 1, 1862. Doc. No. 6, *ibid.*, p. 1013.
[10] Letters of Russell to Scarlett, Nov. 6, Doc. No. 17, and Nov. 7, 1862, Doc. No. 21, *ibid.*, pp. 1026, 1028.

sisted by France and Russia; and in the course of the ensuing battle of diplomatic notes the three Governments were led to define the limitations on national sovereignty implicit in the "guarantee" which they had conferred upon the Kingdom of Greece.

The British Foreign Secretary, as we have seen, recognized the insurrection and flatly refused to intervene in order to mitigate its consequences for the dynasty. Moreover, he warmly applauded the proposed convocation of a constituent assembly for the purpose of framing a new constitution and selecting a new king. But while he disclaimed any intention to influence the Greek people's choice, he reminded the Greek Government that by the agreements of 1830 and 1832 "between England, France, and Russia, no person connected with the Royal or Imperial Families of either [sic] of the powers could be placed on the throne of Greece."[11] He addressed the same reminder to the French and Russian Governments, called their attention to the fact that the promise of the powers not to seek "exclusive influence" went back to the St. Petersburg Protocol of April 4, 1826, which initiated their concerted action in Greece, strongly urged that there should be no departure from this principle even by common consent, and suggested that a joint *démarche* should be undertaken in Athens with a view to forestalling the choice of a King "connected with" any one of the three reigning houses.[12] He proposed, in short, to invoke the self-denying pledge of the protecting powers as a curb on the freedom of Greece in selecting a new ruler; and at the same time he wanted this pledge to be construed so broadly as to exclude any candidates who might be undesirable from the point of view of British interests.

This proposal was opposed by France and Russia, though,

---

[11] Letter of Russell to Scarlett, Nov. 6, 1862, Doc. No. 20, *ibid.*, p. 1028.
[12] Letters of Russell to Lord Napier, British Minister in St. Petersburgh, Nov. 15, 1862, Doc. No. 40, *ibid.*, p. 1042—(Note: "A similar dispatch to Lord Cowley.") —and Nov. 17, 1862, Doc. No. 46, *ibid.*, p. 1051. Letter of Nov. 15, also Doc. No. LXVII in Strupp, ed., *La Situation internationale de la Grèce (1821–1917)*, pp. 163–64.

obviously, for different reasons. Napoleon III, whose rule originated in revolution, was consolidated by a *coup d'état,* and was confirmed by a plebiscite, could hardly have failed to sympathize with an insurrection which had deposed a legitimate dynasty. Moreover, when he was not hampered by a conflict between his principles and his political interests (as, for example, in the Roman question), he showed himself a sincere democrat and an ardent champion of national self-determination; and he could uphold these principles quite unreservedly in connection with the Greek crisis because, unlike Great Britain, he had never regarded Greece as a field of primary importance for French foreign policy. He therefore instructed Drouyn de Lhuys, his Foreign Minister, to reply to Lord Russell that while his Government would be willing to participate in a joint *démarche* calling the Greek Government's attention to the self-denying ordinance which the three powers had imposed upon themselves when they established the Greek monarchy, it could not "indefinitely refuse to recognize a prince whom the Greek nation, without taking these declarations into account, might elect by its free suffrage." For the position of the three powers with respect to Greece was no longer the same as it was in 1830. At that time, they were acting "by virtue of an explicit mandate from Greece when they selected a king. They were therefore able to place certain restrictions on their choice and thus formally to exclude certain candidacies." In 1862, however, Greece was exercising her rights "directly"; and it would be "a denial of these rights," and hence "contrary to the public law of France," to coerce the Greek Government into excluding this or that candidature by threatening to withhold recognition of a ruler elected by the sovereign Greek people simply because his election contravened "agreements made by the powers among themselves."[13]

Unlike Napoleonic France, Russia was as vitally interested in Greece as was Great Britain; and Prince Gortchakoff, the Rus-

[13] Letter of Drouyn de Lhuys, French Foreign Minister, to Cowley, Nov. 20, 1862, with Annex—Verbal Note, Doc. No. LXIX, *ibid.,* pp. 165–66.

sian Chancellor, viewed the Greek crisis as another of the periodic tests of strength between the two great powers which were contending for mastery in the Near East throughout most of the nineteenth century. Because he did not love Otho, he was at first inclined to concede "the right of the Greek people to determine their own destinies."[14] But neither did he relish the violent defiance of constituted authority in the name of popular sovereignty. Hence, his gratification over the deposition of an obstinately Catholic king from the throne of an Orthodox nation was tempered with regret because the removal had been effected through recourse to insurrection. In his conversations with the British Ambassador in St. Petersburg and in his instructions to the Russian Ambassador in London he "animadverted with some austerity" on "the principles of popular right" which had been invoked by Lord Russell to justify the insurrection; and shrewdly discerning the main reason of the British Foreign Secretary's sympathy with it, he "contrasted unfavorably the character of revolutionary agencies and of the revolutionary authorities in Greece with that of the instruments of the English Revolution of 1688."[15] With regard to the British proposal of a joint *démarche* at Athens, the Russian Chancellor was obdurate. He objected that to rule out the candidacy of any prince "connected with" the three royal houses "would exclude all the princes in Europe, who are all connected," would make it impossible for the Greeks to find a king, "cast them into disorder and drive them into republican notions or to the choice of a native sovereign who would have no authority in the country." He pointed out that the terms of exclusion in the original treaty were of a "more distinct and limited character"; but he indicated that even if the defect of the British proposal on this score were remedied, he would still refuse to make "the desired declaration by anticipation in Athens," because, apart from its possible disastrous consequences, such a step would be inconsistent with the position

[14] Letter of Napier to Russell, Nov. 4, 1862, Doc. LXVa, *ibid.*, pp. 161–62.
[15] Letter of Napier to Russell, Nov. 19, 1862, Doc. No. 65, B.F.S.P., LVIII, 1065.

already taken by Lord Russell toward the Greek insurrection. For whereas in his first dispatch his Lordship "recognized the principle of popular sovereignty and opened a wide field of freedom to the Greeks," he now "proposed to subject them to premature restrictions."[16]

Having laid himself open to a lecture by both Napoleon III and Prince Gortchakoff on the meaning of popular sovereignty, the British Foreign Secretary did not press his original proposal.[17] But the further unfolding of Russian policy permitted him to return to the charge more directly. "The obligations of treaties and rights still existing," said the Russian Chancellor to the British Ambassador, "must be respected and not lightly cast aside." Starting from this premise, he proposed to ask the Bavarian Government "whether they still claimed their rights under the existing treaties having reference to Greece"; and if they did, "whether they had a prince ready, in the conditions of the treaty, professing the Greek faith." The Greek throne would be considered vacant only "in case the Government of Bavaria abandoned their rights" or "if they did not abandon their rights but gave a hesitating or evasive reply on the question of religion," since the effect of such a reply would be to "annul" the succession. "But if a Bavarian prince was brought forward, fulfilling all the conditions of the existing treaties, and especially the stipulations regarding religion, then the Russian Government would offer the prince to the Greek nation, without peremptorily pressing or imposing him."[18] In short, the Russian Chancellor based the defense of a fundamental Russian interest—the placing of an Orthodox king on the throne of Greece—on the principles of legitimacy and the sanctity of treaties; but in order to strengthen his case, he did not hesitate to invoke also, somewhat incongruously, the primacy of the

---

[16] Letters of Napier to Russell, Nov. 14, 1862, Doc. No. 53, and Nov. 19, 1862, Doc. No. 65, *ibid.*, pp. 1054, 1062–63.
[17] Letter of Russell to Cowley, Nov. 24, 1862, Doc. No. 57, *ibid.*, p. 1057. Also Doc. No. LXXI in Strupp, ed., *op. cit.*, p. 167.
[18] Letters of Napier to Russell, Nov. 19, 1862, Doc. No. 65, and Dec. 7, 1862, Doc. No. 106, B.F.S.P., LVIII, 1063, 1099.

national will with respect to the religion of the future kings of Greece as embodied in the Constitution of 1844 and internationally recognized by the London Treaty of November 20, 1852.

What made the declaration of Russian policy ominous to the British Government was the fact that a candidate who could meet all these qualifications was known to be available. The Duke of Leuchtenberg, son of the daughter of the late Czar Nicholas, was "a Russian subject by birth, residence, baptism, and official declaration"; but he was "possibly also" a Bavarian subject "according to the laws of Bavaria, in virtue of his Bavarian father and his Bavarian title."[19] The facts that he belonged to the Orthodox Church and that he was created Prince Romanoffsky shortly after the ratification of Article XL of the Greek Constitution by international agreement[20] gave rise to the suspicion that he was being groomed as Russia's candidate for the succession of King Otho. And this suspicion was confirmed by Prince Gortchakoff's violent objection to Lord Russell's broad construction of the self-denying pledge of the three powers. For the extension of the ban to all princes "connected with" any of the three dynasties would obviously rule out the candidacy of the Duke of Leuchtenberg even if he and his sponsors were able to prove that he was not immediately related to the Russian imperial family.

Blandly assuming that the candidacy of the Duke of Leuchtenberg would be sponsored by Russia, Lord Russell proceeded to state the British attitude toward such a contingency in unambiguous language. He contended that even if a less inclusive wording (than "connected with") were to be substituted for his proposed terms of exclusion, they would still apply to Russia's putative candidate.

[19] Letter of Napier to Russell, Nov. 20, 1862, Doc. No. 66, *ibid.*, pp. 1066–67.
[20] Ukase of the Czar to the Governing Senate, Dec. 21, 1852. Inclosure 2 with Letter of Napier to Russell, Nov. 20, 1862, Doc. No. 66, *ibid.*, p. 1068, and Treaty of the Three Protecting Powers with Bavaria and Greece, London, Nov. 20, 1862, *ibid.*, XLI, 36. See also Letter of Russell to Napier, Nov. 28, 1862, Doc. No. 69, *ibid.*, LVIII, 1070, and Letter of Russell to Cowley Dec. 3, 1862, Doc. No. 84, *ibid.*, p. 1080.

As a question of policy [he added] I desire to state to Prince Gortchakoff that Her Majesty's Government . . . have no desire to see an English Prince on the throne of Greece, but that we have insurmountable objections to seeing a Russian Prince on that throne; that his being King of Greece would place us in direct antagonism with Greece, . . . and in fact would greatly endanger the peace of Europe.

And he concluded with the solemn warning that the British Government would "take every fair and honorable means to prevent the Duke of Leuchtenberg from becoming King of Greece."[21]

The Russian Chancellor could afford to yield to this threat, because he had won what he considered an important point. Though he probably had not intended to push the Duke's candidacy, by encouraging the belief that he did he had elicited from the British Government a self-denying pledge with respect to Prince Alfred. As he had strongly suspected the sincerity of British protestations of disinterestedness and had complained to the British Ambassador that the Prince's election (to the throne of Greece) "was agitated and impelled" by the British consular authorities and "in a variety of ways,"[22] he was the more gratified to receive from the British Foreign Secretary direct and binding assurance on this score. He therefore instructed the Russian Ambassador in London to declare to Lord Russell that the Russian Government acknowledged the validity of the commitment concerning the exclusion of members of the three reigning houses; and that, consequently, it was ready to enter with the British Government into a "mutual agreement" whereby both the Duke of Leuchtenberg and Prince Alfred would be excluded in case they were called to the throne of Greece "by the wishes of the Greek nation."[23] This proposal amounted to acceptance of the British thesis that under the self-denying pledge of the three powers, the putative Russian

[21] Letter of Russell to Napier, Nov. 28, 1862, Doc. No. 69, *ibid.*, p. 1071.
[22] Letter of Napier to Russell, Nov. 22, 1862, Doc. No. 76, *ibid.*, p. 1077.
[23] Letter of Baron Brunnow, Russian Ambassador at London, to Russell, Dec. 4, 1862, Doc. No. 85, *ibid.*, p. 1081.

candidate was quite as ineligible to the Greek throne as was the English prince. The way was therefore cleared for a joint declaration to the Greek Government, though much more restricted in scope than that originally proposed by the British Foreign Secretary. Instead of a blanket ban on all candidates "connected with" the three dynasties, the protecting powers notified Greece that the exclusion clause of the Protocol of February 3, 1830, applied specifically to the Duke of Leuchtenberg and to Prince Alfred, and that they were therefore precluded from consideration as candidates to the throne vacated by King Otho's deposition.[24]

By this declaration a major objective of British policy was attained. For the British Government was determined not to allow an English prince to ascend the throne of Greece. It knew, even before it was told by an authorized Greek spokesman, that Prince Alfred's election was associated in the minds of the Greek people with a "patient expectation that . . . Thessaly and Epirus on the one side, and the Ionian Islands, on the other, might be peacefully united to the Greek Kingdom."[25] It agreed with the French Foreign Minister's grave warning[26] that the intimate association of the English royal house with the struggling Hellenic kingdom was intended and in the end would be bound to commit Great Britain, the staunchest defender of the Ottoman Empire, to the support of Greek Irredentism, the most persistent threat to that Empire's territorial integrity. Yet, however unpleasant this prospect, the accession of a Russian prince was an even more unpalatable alternative. For it would enhance Russian influence in Greece; and since Russia was notoriously not committed to the integrity of the Ottoman Empire, it might provide the land-starved little king-

---

[24] Joint Note of the Three Protecting Powers to the Provisional Government, Dec. 13, 1862, Inclosure with Letter of Scarlett to Russell, Dec. 15, 1862, Doc. No. 124, *ibid.*, p. 1107.

[25] Letter of Russell to Scarlett, Nov. 29, 1862, Doc. No. 74, *ibid.*, p. 1075.

[26] Circular dispatch of De Lhuys to the Diplomatic agents of France, Dec. 4, 1862, Inclosure in letter of Napier to Russell, Dec. 26, 1862, Doc. No. 134, *ibid.*, pp. 1113–18. Also Doc. LXXIV in Strupp, ed., *op. cit.*, p. 174.

dom with sufficient Russian assistance to encourage an effectively aggressive foreign policy. Hence, the removal of both of these unpleasant alternatives through Russia's consent to consider the Duke of Leuchtenberg equally ineligible with Prince Alfred, was a diplomatic victory for Great Britain; and her position of virtual primacy among the three protecting powers was further strengthened by the overwhelming majority which Prince Alfred secured in the plebiscite that was held despite the reminder concerning his ineligibility.[27]

The prince's election, though obviously invalid, was not without significance. For it was an expression of the naïve and unlimited faith of the Greek people in British beneficence; and it placed the vacant throne of Greece, as it were, in Britain's special keeping. In response to this gesture the British Government discharged its obligations of guardianship by taking the intiative in all the subsequent transactions connected with the settlement of the dynastic and constitutional crisis, by eventually selecting for Greece a prince who was—and remained throughout his long reign—peculiarly susceptible to British influence, and by associating his accession with the annexation of the Ionian Islands—a long overdue sop to the Irredentist aspirations of the Greek people and a timely bid for their good will toward the new dynasty.

Lord Russell's diplomatic victory spurred Prince Gortchakoff to new efforts. His policy, as we have seen, was motivated by reluctance to legitimatize the violent overthrow of a dynastic settlement made by international agreement and by his desire to avail himself of the expulsion of Otho in order to place an Orthodox king on the throne of Greece. Having been compelled to rule out the Duke of Leuchtenberg, he sought to accomplish both his ends by appealing to two documents— the Treaty of May 7, 1832, which, "under the guarantee of the three Courts," invested Prince Otho of Bavaria with the

---

[27] Letter of Scarlett to Russell, Dec. 17, 1862, Doc. No. 126, B.F.S.P., LVIII, 1107–8. Cf. *The Cambridge History of British Foreign Policy*, II, 609; and Finlay, *A History of Greece*, VII, 286n.

"hereditary sovereignty of Greece," and the Treaty of November 20, 1852, which ratified the stipulation of Article XL of the Greek Constitution imposing on King Otho's successor adherence to the Orthodox faith. But when it was pointed out to him that "the Greeks were free to modify Article XL of their Constitution, as they could alter any other article," that the Treaty of 1852 "had merely reference to the presumed succession of King Otho in the ordinary way," and that it could not "be held to apply to a new sovereign of another family,"[28] he retreated from his position. He admitted that the religious question was the domestic concern of the Greek people, but hinted that the stipulation of the Treaty of 1852 should be reaffirmed since it was "substantially based" on the conviction of the protecting powers "that the tie of common religion should exist between the sovereign of Greece and his people."[29]

At the same time, the Russian Chancellor stuck to his original view that the Treaty of May 7, 1832, gave the Bavarian royal family a lien on the throne of Greece (provided always that it accepted the prescription of the Constitution of 1844 and of the Treaty of 1852 on the religious issue). His proposal that a "combined overture" to this effect be made by the three powers to the Bavarian Government had been prompted, he said, "by the respect due to the House of Bavaria and . . . to international engagements."[30] He strongly deprecated the other two powers' haste to accept the annulment of the treaties "concerning the establishment and succession of the Bavarian dynasty . . . by the breath of a popular revolution in Greece." And he argued that "if those treaties were to fall, they might be dissolved in a regular and orderly fashion."[31] This would obviously mean inviting Bavaria (the fourth party to the Treaty of 1832 and the fifth to that of 1852) to negotiate a new agreement. Bavarian and Russian diplomacy worked hard to secure such an invitation; and the British Government was given to

---

[28] Letter of Napier to Russell, Nov. 22, 1862, Doc. No. 75, B.F.S.P., LVIII, 1076.
[29] *Ibid.*
[30] Letter of Napier to Russell, Dec. 7, 1862, Doc. No. 106, *ibid.*, p. 1099.
[31] *Ibid.*

understand that a new settlement was easily feasible on the basis of King Otho's formal abdication in exchange for the retention of the Greek Crown in the Royal House of Bavaria.[32] Such a settlement, however, would imply that King Otho, despite his deposition by an insurrection which presumably reflected the national will, and for all the unanimous confirmation of this action by an Assembly possessing a fresh mandate from the nation, still preserved the rights conferred on him by international treaties and could barter them away for the benefit of his family. The refusal of Great Britain and France to commit themselves to this doctrine practically eliminated Bavaria as a party to the new dynastic settlement. The note which defined the British Government's position, after pointing out that no effort to recall King Otho had been made by the Greek nation since October, 1862, and that no intention had been "manifested in any quarter to attempt restoration by a foreign force," concluded as follows:

> In these circumstances, Her Majesty's Government think it incumbent upon them to state without reserve to the Court of Bavaria that they consider it an urgent and imperative duty on their part to endeavor to replace Greece under a Government conformable to the monarchical principle, which they have an interest to maintain in a state to the foundation of which Great Britain, in concert with other Powers, so greatly contributed.[33]

It appeared then to be the view of the British Government that while the "guarantee" of Britain—and of the other two powers—had lapsed as a safeguard of King Otho and of the Bavarian dynasty, it was still valid with respect to the monarchy and might presumably have been invoked to prevent the establishment of a republic. But since the Greek people remained steadfastly attached to the monarchy,[34] had invited an English

---

[32] Letter of Napier to Russell, Dec. 21, 1862, Doc. No. 121, *ibid.*, p. 1106.
[33] Letter of Russell to Lord A. Loftus, May 16, 1863, Doc. No. 1, *ibid.*, LIV, 38–39.
[34] Proclamation of the Provisional Government of the Kingdom of Greece, Oct. 23, 1862, Inclosure 1 with Letter of Scarlett to Russell, Oct. 24, 1862, Doc, No. 7, *ibid.*, LVIII, 1018.

prince by an overwhelming majority to be their king, and on the British Government's refusal to sanction their choice had commissioned the protecting powers to search for a suitable candidate, the way was clear for restoring in Greece a government "conformable to the monarchical principle," except for a serious legal obstacle. Because King Otho had neither formally abdicated nor renounced all claims of his House to the throne of Greece, it was a measure of elementary precaution on behalf of his successor to supersede the Treaty of May 7, 1832, by an international agreement which should register the dynastic change effected by the insurrection of October, 1862. The Conference of Ambassadors which met in London during the months of May and June, 1863, addressed itself to this task and invited the signatories of the treaty which was about to be interred to attend the obsequies.[35] When the Bavarian Government refused, the representatives of Great Britain, France, and Russia, the other three signatories of the Treaty of May 7, 1832, proceeded to declare it terminated. At their meeting on May 27, 1863, they decided to insert in the Protocol the reservations made by the Bavarian Government (in accordance with Article VIII of the Treaty) in favor of minor branches of the Bavarian dynasty. But they immediately added that the stipulations of Article VIII were impossible to execute owing to "an event of *force majeure*" for which the protecting powers were in no way responsible; and that the three Governments, considering themselves "released from their mandate by circumstances which the Convention of 1832 had not foreseen," could not indefinitely delay placing the Kingdom of Greece, "which had been founded by their united efforts," under a new dynastic regime.[36] They accordingly invited to their next meeting a representative of the Danish Government in order to make the necessary treaty arrangements for the accession of Prince William of

---

[35] Protocol (1), London, May 16, 1863, *ibid.*, LIII, 144–45. Also Doc. No. LXXVI in Strupp, ed., *op. cit.*, pp. 176–77.

[36] Protocol (2), London, May 27, 1863, B.F.S.P., LIII, 145–46. Also Doc. No. LXXVII in Strupp, ed., *op. cit.*, pp. 177–78.

Denmark, who had been called to the throne of Greece by decision of the Greek nation.[37]

III

This procedure differed essentially from that followed in 1832, when the Greek people merely ratified the choice of the protecting powers after giving them a mandate to select a king. No such authority was delegated to the powers in 1862. The decree of October 23, which deposed King Otho, entrusted the task of finding a successor to a National Assembly, the first part of whose mandate was the framing of a new constitution.[38]

The throne [wrote the well-informed British Minister in Athens to his chief] will be offered to a Prince ready and willing to subscribe to the conditions of the constitution. . . . It is for this reason alone that the election of a sovereign is not to precede the establishment of the constitution under which he is to reign.[39]

In point of fact it was found impossible to maintain this order of precedence. Yet the procedure that was followed in the election of King Otho's successor removed the constitutional ambiguities of the Othonian regime. The insurrection of 1862, by laying down the principles that the new monarch should be called to the throne by the voice of the people and that his authority should be derivative and limited, that is, confined to the powers conferred upon him by a constitution in the making of which he was not to participate, intended to leave no doubt as to the location of sovereignty in the Greek state. These principles were not deviated from throughout the crisis. The National Assembly's Decree of February 5, 1863, which unanimously confirmed the plebiscitary election of Prince Alfred, stated significantly that he had been "elected constitutional

[37] Protocol (3), London, June 5, 1863, B.F.S.P., LIII, 146–48. Also Doc. No. LXXVIII in Strupp, ed., *op. cit.*, pp. 178–79.
[38] Proclamation of the Provisional Government, Oct. 23, 1862, Inclosure 1 with Letter of Scarlett to Russell, Oct. 24, 1862, Doc. No. 7, B.F.S.P., LVIII, 1017. See also Letter of Scarlett to Russell, Nov. 8, 1862, Doc. No. 44, *ibid.*, p. 1050. Cf. Finlay, *A History of Greece*, VII, 315.
[39] Letter of Scarlett to Russell, Nov. 8, 1862, Doc. No. 44, B.F.S.P., LVIII, 1050.

king of the Greeks by the sovereign will of the nation."[40] And when Great Britain, invoking the Prince's ineligibility of which the protecting powers had already reminded Greece, vetoed his election, the Assembly authorized its commission on foreign affairs to coöperate with the Government in the search for another candidate. The Government in turn appealed to the protecting powers, especially to Great Britain, for guidance. But this mandate, unlike that of 1832, was strictly limited.[41]

We have not received [declared Lord Palmerston, the British Prime Minister] plenary power from the [Greek] people to select a sovereign for them. They are to exercise their own choice. All the British Government can do is to suggest a person who may appear fitting on the one hand, and whom they would be likely to accept on the other.[42]

The search (in which Lord Palmerston took a lively personal interest) was rapidly concluded. And when the Greek Government announced to the Assembly that the new candidate was Prince William of Denmark, it stressed his "constitutional upbringing" and recommended his unanimous election on the strength of indications that he would respect the law of the land and make a good "constitutional king." He was thereupon elected by acclamation; and a decree of the Assembly named him "constitutional King of the Hellenes," under the name of George I, stipulated that his heirs must profess the Eastern Orthodox faith, and instructed a delegation of three (of which Admiral Kanares was appointed chairman) to proceed to Copenhagen in order to offer him the crown on behalf of the Greek nation.[43]

Thus the doctrine of national sovereignty was affirmed both in the deposition of the first dynasty and in the accession of the

---

[40] Finlay, *A History of Greece,* VII, 286.

[41] *Ibid.,* p. 287, and Driault, *op. cit.,* III, 55–57.

[42] Lord Palmerston in the House of Commons, March 16, 1863, Hansard, comp., *Parliamentary Debates,* CLXIX, 1530.

[43] Decree of the National Assembly, March 30, 1863, B.F.S.P., LIV, 39–40. See also Letter of Sir A. Paget to Earl Russell, June 6, 1863, Doc. No. 2, *ibid.,* pp. 39–40. Cf. Finlay, *A History of Greece,* VII, 292.

second. Whereas King Otho was chosen by the protecting powers by virtue of a mandate they had received from insurgent Greece and immediately transferred to himself the sovereignty of the nation, his successor was elected by a National Assembly after it had been reassured concerning his political tendencies, and was pointedly designated *"constitutional* King of the Hellenes." That he and his advisers understood this designation to be an essential condition attached to the offer of the crown was clearly intimated when in his speech of acceptance he stressed the fact that he had been "born and educated in a country in which the rule of law went hand in hand with true constitutional liberty."[44] Moreover, unlike the Treaty of May 7, 1832, which was negotiated without consultation with the Greek people, the Treaty of July 13, 1863, by which Denmark and the protecting powers established the second dynastic regime of Greece, adhered to the conditions laid down by the National Assembly and recognized the primacy of the national will in the constitutional field. In compliance with the decree of the Assembly already alluded to, it conferred on him the title "King of the Hellenes," declared Greece (under the "guarantee" of the protecting powers) "a monarchical, independent and *constitutional* state," stipulated that his heirs must belong to the Eastern Orthodox Church, and (unlike the Treaty of 1832 which regulated King Otho's majority) recognized the National Assembly's right to terminate his minority before the actual attainment of the age of eighteen prescribed by the Danish dynastic law.[45] Finally, by the Treaty of March 29, 1864, which registered the annexation of the Ionian Islands to Greece, the protecting powers reaffirmed their "guarantee" in identical terms with those of the Treaty of July 3, 1863. Thus the international arrangements which attended the installation of the Gluecksburg dynasty complied with—instead of dictating to—

---

[44] Reply of the King of the Hellenes to a Greek Delegation, Inclosure with Letter of Sir A. Paget to Russell, June 6, 1863, Doc. No. 2, B.F.S.P., LIV, 42.
[45] Article III, Treaty between Great Britain, France and Russia, with Denmark, relative to the accession of Prince William of Denmark to the Throne of Greece, London, July 13, 1863, B.F.S.P., LIII, 28–31.

the national will. They recognized both the dynastic change effected by the insurrection of October, 1862, and the will of the nation to live under a constitution; and they stretched the "guarantee" of the powers to cover also the "constitutionality" of the Greek state, thus establishing the legal basis for their drastic intervention during the World War.

But while the protecting powers conceded to the Greek people the right to tear up an international agreement which regulated the dynastic status of Greece and substantially deferred to the national will in making the new dynastic settlement, they stoutly upheld the immutability of treaties in so far as they affected their immediate interests. The treaty which placed Otho on the throne of Greece was dead. Yet Article XI of its successor provided that "the accession of Prince William to the Greek throne shall in no way modify the financial obligations undertaken by Greece by virtue of Article XII of the London Treaty of May 7, 1832." The Greek Government could reasonably claim that since these obligations were defined in a treaty signed by Bavaria and the protecting powers and were the financial concomitant of the establishment of the first dynasty, need for a revision of their most onerous features at the time of the accession of the second dynasty was strongly indicated. Needless to say, no such revision was made, even though, as we have seen, Article XII of the Treaty of May 7, 1832, seriously impaired the sovereignty of the Greek state.[46] The insurrection of October, 1862, successfully asserted the right of national self-determination in the dynastic and constitutional fields; but the financial obligations to which Greece had been committed by four foreign Governments retained their full rigor even after the violent overthrow of the regime which had contracted them on her behalf.

The primacy of national sovereignty was also recognized by the Assembly when it finally addressed itself to its second important task—the framing of a new constitution. The resolution

---

[46] Article XI, Treaty of July 13, 1863, *ibid.*, p. 30; and Article XII, Treaty of May 7, 1832, *ibid.*, XIX, 38–39.

of October 22, 1863, which defined the authority of the King during the interval between his accession and the going into effect of the new constitutional charter, transferred to him "the royal prerogatives and the executive power" as defined in the Constitution of 1844 in so far as they did not conflict with the decrees issued since the insurrection of October, 1862. The same resolution made all the measures enacted by the Assembly in its legislative capacity subject to the royal veto; but it expressly exempted the constitution and thus excluded the Crown from the concurrent exercise of the constituent power.[47] In his first address to the nation King George indicated his acquiescence in these arrangements. Unlike his predecessor, who called himself "by the grace of God King of Greece," he acknowledged that he had been called to the throne by the will of the Greek people and pledged himself to faithful observance of the laws and "above all of the Constitution, the cornerstone of the new Hellenic polity."[48]

But while the King accepted the principle of non-interference with the constituent functions of the Assembly, he was compelled by its dilatoriness and the growing restlessness of public opinion to intervene decisively in order to expedite the restoration of political normality. In a message addressed to the Assembly in October, 1864, he called attention to the anomaly created by the concentration of both the legislative and the constituent power in the same body, submitted a draft (countersigned by the ministers) of Articles LXXIII–CVII, which comprised the unfinished part of the Constitution, and peremptorily demanded that the Assembly wind up its labors within ten days or shoulder the responsibility for the consequences.[49] Confronted by this thinly veiled threat of abdication, the Assembly rejected a motion to debate the King's right to intervene and speeded up its work in order to comply with the time limit

---

[47] Resolution of the Greek Assembly, Oct. 22, 1863.
[48] Proclamation of King George to the Greek Nation, October 1863, *ibid.*, LIV, 50.
[49] Message of King George to the National Assembly, Oct. 6 (18), 1864, *ibid.*, LV, 886–87. See also Driault, *op. cit.*, III, 94.

set by the royal ultimatum. At the same time, by refusing to substitute the King's draft for that of its own committee, it showed its determination to resist all attempts to encroach on its constituent functions. It is true that it adopted, by a majority of only one vote, Articles LXXXIII, LXXXIV, LXXXV, and LXXXVI of the royal draft, which revived the early Othonian institution of the Council of State. But so strong was the opposition that the stipulation was made (in Article CVIII) that the articles in question could be revised by a three-fourths vote of the Chamber of Deputies; and a resolution abolishing the Council of State was accordingly passed at the next parliamentary session and was signed and promulgated as law by the King.[50] When the completed Constitution was submitted to the King, he requested reconsideration of Article II, which made Greek citizenship compulsory for the secular clergy of the Roman Catholic Church, and of Article CVII, which dealt with the subject of revision. With regard to the first of the disputed articles, the issue was raised by the French Government's claim that it violated the London Protocol of February 3, 1830, which guaranteed civil and religious liberty to Roman Catholics. The Assembly, recognizing that the Crown could legitimately concern itself with constitutional matters when they impinged on the domain of foreign policy, amended the article in question so as to make it conform to the international obligations assumed by Greece contemporaneously with the recognition of her independence. But it refused to yield on Article CVII (which prescribed a rather complicated amending process) and advanced the excuse that it had been unable to find a more satisfactory version.[51]

IV

The Constitution of 1864, so far as it was founded on experience, was inspired by the object lesson of the emasculation and the distortion of its predecessor into an instrument of monarchical autocracy. In order to avert a repetition of that failure, it

[50] Article CVIII, Constitution of 1864, Finlay, *A History of Greece*, VII, 357.
[51] Article CVII, *ibid.*, p. 356.

abolished the Senate, which had proved a prolific source of autocratic power under the Othonian regime, and it attempted to remove a basic misunderstanding concerning the location of sovereignty which had vitiated the constitutional development of the Hellenic state ever since it was founded on a monarchical basis. This was the purpose of the declaration of Article XXI that "all powers are derived from the nation and are exercised in the manner prescribed by the constitution." The new Constitution was not, in other words, like its predecessor, even theoretically a compact between the sovereign monarch and the nation, but an instrument of government devised by a sovereign people, which defined the status and the powers of the Crown as merely one of the several agencies of the state. As the late Professor N. N. Saripolos, its foremost Greek commentator, has pointed out, it was based on a more advanced literary theory.[52] The ostensibly voluntary surrender of some of the authority of the sovereign monarch, which was recorded in the Constitution of 1844, was intended to establish a regime of limited monarchy. But the self-limitation of the sovereign people through the Constitution of 1864 was designed to create a limited democracy, in effect a "royal republic,"[53] with a chief of state enjoying lifelong and hereditary tenure, but exercising (in the words of Article XLIV) "no other powers than those explicitly conferred upon him by the constitution and the special laws made in pursuance thereto."

The fact that these powers did not include a share in the amending process is conclusive evidence of the subordinate position of the Crown and of the derivative character of its authority under the Constitution of 1864. While the legislative power was vested in the king and Parliament, revision of the "non-fundamental" clauses of the constitution could only be initiated by Parliament and carried through by a specially elected revisionist Assembly.[54] The King could neither prevent

[52] Nikolaos N. Saripolos, The Public Law of Greece, I, 56, 62–65, as cited by Couclelis, Les Régimes gouvernementaux de la Grèce . . ., p. 97.
[53] Article XLIV, Finlay, A History of Greece, VII, 350.
[54] Articles XXII and CVII, ibid., pp. 348, 356.

the initiation of amendments, since the annual convocation of Parliament was constitutionally prescribed, nor postpone their enactment, as with ordinary legislation, through the exercise of the veto power.[55] His share in the revision—as in the original framing—of the Constitution was confined to the formality of signing and promulgation, which was construed to mean not ratification, that is, consent, but acceptance.[56] Thus thirty-two years after the last Assembly of the revolutionary period was prevented by the ministers of the protecting powers from drawing up a constitution without the collaboration of the king,[57] another Assembly of revolutionary origin was able to produce a monarchical constitution founded on the principle that the constituent power belongs to the sovereign nation.

[55] Article XXXVII, *ibid.,* p. 349.
[56] Article CIX, *ibid.,* p. 357, and Article XLIII, *ibid.,* p. 348.
[57] Article XXI, *ibid.,* p. 348. See also p. 90, *supra.*

Chapter Seven

THE WORLD WAR AND THE CONSTITUTIONAL CRISIS IN GREECE

I

THE CRISIS of 1909–1911 did not involve the protecting powers —the third party to the constitutional development of modern Greece—and is therefore outside the scope of this study. Nevertheless, it deserves brief consideration because it provided the occasion for the only relatively orderly revision of the constitution since the founding of the Greek state and was the prelude to the fateful conflict which arose four years later over the question of Greek participation in the World War. It began in August, 1909, with the sudden incursion into Greek politics of the so-called Military League—a group of mostly subaltern army and navy officers who staged a mutiny of the Athens garrison and demanded a series of drastic reforms beginning with the removal from the army of Crown Prince Constantine and the other members of the royal family. Though partly motivated by personal ambition and considerations of professional preferment, the action of the Military League reflected also profound popular discontent with both the international situation and the internal condition of Greece. Deeply wounded by the humiliating defeat of 1897, national sentiment had become increasingly exacerbated by the inability of Greek diplomacy to cope with the pressing problems of foreign policy created by the Young Turk insurrection of 1908, the rapid progress of rival Balkan Irredentisms in Macedonia at the expense of Hellenism, the Cretan question, and the indifference or hostility of the European powers. The failure of Greece to make her weight felt in the field of international relations, and the slow pace of her domestic progress in comparison with that of other

Balkan states prompted anxious questionings about many aspects of Neo-Hellenic culture and produced a significant literature of criticism and revolt, the most obvious targets of which were the political leaders and parties, the parliamentary system, the dynasty, and the monarchy itself. The suggestive theory that this *malaise* was symptomatic of a somewhat belated drive of the Greek middle class for political power is perhaps too simple an explanation of a complex phenomenon. It is nevertheless true that the new ferment was prevalent in the urban centers, that it affected the mercantile and professional classes and the more advanced intelligentsia, and that it finally crystallized into a revolt of "new men," that is, a younger generation of mostly middle-class politicians, against the oligarchy of quasi-hereditary sectional clans which had managed to retain throughout the nineteenth century a disproportionate share of political power.

This movement, which was anti-oligarchic, anti-dynastic, potentially republican, and intensely nationalistic, was diverted by Eleutherios Venizelos into the relatively harmless channel of constitutional revision; and having thus been made to shed its violence, it applied its energies to the unprecedently constructive effort made by the Greek nation under the leadership of the Cretan statesman during the brief period which preceded the outbreak of the World War. Mr. Venizelos's recommendation to the Military League when he was called to Athens in December, 1909, as its political adviser, was that it should dissolve itself after obtaining from the Government a promise that it would sponsor the revision of the constitution. This policy was eventually adopted by George I and the majority of political leaders. The amending process was initiated (on March 3, 1910) by a vote of more than the required three-fourths of the Chamber of Deputies, which was thereupon dissolved. It was succeeded (in accordance with Article CVII of the Constitution) by a Revisionist Assembly at the opening meeting of which the Dragoumis Ministry—the third since the outbreak of the military revolt—submitted its resignation. After a ministerial crisis which lasted a week and showed conclusively that the old political leaders were unwilling or unable to govern under the new dispensation, Mr. Venizelos was invited (on October 18, 1910) to form his first Government. He immediately dissolved the Assembly, although it had given him a somewhat grudging vote of confidence; and in the ensuing general election he secured a resounding victory which enabled him in less than six months to push through the second Revisionist Assembly fifty-four amendments to the Constitution of 1864 and thus to terminate in June, 1911, the political crisis precipitated in August, 1909, by the revolutionary action of the Military League.

Though this revision professedly followed the elaborate amending process prescribed by Article CVII, it deviated from it in certain essential points. In the first place, it did not originate in the Chamber of Deputies, except as a matter of the merest formality. In point of fact, it was initiated by extra-parliamentary pressure and was decided upon at a meeting of political leaders presided over by the King. It thus violated the literal theory of the Constitution of 1864 which excluded the Crown from the exercise of the constituent power. Moreover, the resolution to amend the Constitution was passed by the Chamber of Deputies only once instead of in two successive sessions; and there was considerable divergence between the amendments it proposed and those that were finally enacted.[1] At the same time, the revision did adhere to Article CVII in that it was scrupulously confined to the "non-fundamental" provisions of the constitution. It thus achieved the essentially conservative purpose of its chief sponsors, King George I and Mr. Venizelos, who used it as a sop designed to emasculate the potentially revolutionary movement of August, 1909. From this initially anti-dynastic crisis, thanks largely to Mr. Venizelos's masterly handling, the monarchy emerged with renewed strength. And when King George's successor added to the ample consti-

---

[1] Constitution of the Kingdom of Greece, October, 1862, revised by the Second Revisionist Assembly, June 1, 1911, Strupp, ed., *La Situation internationale de la Grèce* . . ., pp. 250-56; see especially the Amendments.

tutional prerogatives of the Crown (which had been left intact by the revision of 1911), the popularity of a victorious war lord and the mystical promise of the name Constantine, the stage was set for the struggle between the King and the Prime Minister which ushered in the longest revolutionary cycle in the history of modern Greece.

II

The subordination of the domestic development of Greece to the exigencies of her international situation was conclusively demonstrated during the political and constitutional crisis which was precipitated by the World War. What aggravated this crisis was the peculiar position of the Crown as the supreme arbiter of foreign policy. The traditional identification of the dynasty with the state, and the concomitant leadership of the Crown in international relations was a potent reality until the outbreak of the World War even in the constitutionally governed countries of Western Europe. In the newly created Balkan states, especially in Greece, the most dependent of all on the good will of the European powers, the potency of dynastic ties was so unquestioningly assumed that the conception of the Crown as a court of last appeal in the conduct of foreign policy had come to be recognized as one of the conventions of the constitution. It was therefore inevitable that the divergence of opinion on the question of the entry of Greece into the War should resolve itself into a conflict between the King, who claimed to be the authentic voice of that mystic entity, the nation, and the Prime Minister, who was the leader of the ephemeral parliamentary majority in a constitutional state.

Granted that the strict letter of the Constitution set no limits to the right of the King to "appoint and dismiss his ministers," and to dissolve parliament, should not this power be qualified by the basic assumptions of constitutional government founded on the principle of popular sovereignty? To this question, which sums up the constitutional issue between King Constantine and Mr. Venizelos, the practice of the preceding half century of constitutional government afforded a fairly clear answer. During the first ten years of his reign King George I, undeterred by the fate of his predecessor, attempted to govern through minority or extra-parliamentary ministries on behalf of which he made lavish use of the weapon of dissolution. The consequences of this ill-advised course were ministerial instability, scandalous governmental interference with elections, administrative paralysis and corruption, and an alarming increase of anti-dynastic sentiment due to the fact that the Crown was closely identified with the successive ministries and was therefore held responsible for their lawlessness and incompetence. These unmistakable storm-signals proved an effective warning; and when the ministry headed by Demetrios Voulgaris, the worst offender against constitutional government, resigned in May, 1875, the King displayed almost for the first time that sagacity which distinguished him both from his predecessor and from his successor and called to the premiership Charilaos Tricoupis, who had been an outspoken critic of his unconstitutional course. But while it was true that the combination of minority or extra-parliamentary ministries with frequent dissolutions had resulted substantially in monarchical absolutism, the principle laid down by the new Prime Minister, according to which no party or group leader should be invited to form a ministry unless he enjoyed the "declared" (δεδηλωμένη) confidence of the majority of Parliament,[2] would nullify the Crown's right to dissolve by depriving it of the *means* of dissolution, and would thus tend to establish a parliamentary tyranny during the four-year term of each Parliament.[3] In point of fact, neither Tricoupis nor Alexander Koumoundouros, who shares with him the distinction of having consolidated constitutional and parliamentary government in Greece, insisted on strict adherence to this principle. Throughout the reign of George I the King's legal right to dissolve the Chamber of Deputies through a minority ministry was recognized; but it was understood that dissolution should be resorted to in order to bring Parliament into

---

[2] Couclelis, *Les Régimes gouvernementaux de la Grèce de 1821 à nos jours*, p. 112.   [3] *Ibid.*, p. 113.

harmony with the will of the nation rather than as a means of promoting the policies advocated by the Crown.[4]

Hence, after Mr. Venizelos had resigned in March, 1915 (despite his parliamentary majority), because he had been unable to secure King Constantine's consent to Greek participation in the Gallipoli campaign, the King acted in accordance with both the law and the custom of the constitution when he called to the premiership Demetrios Gounaris, one of the leaders of the opposition and decreed the dissolution of the Chamber of Deputies. For he thereby exercised one of the most important functions of the Crown—that of initiating an appeal from the representatives of the nation to the nation itself; an appeal the more urgent because it involved the vital issue of war and peace, which had arisen since the election of the last Parliament. But though the Liberal (Venizelist) Party won the general election of June 13, 1915, by a reduced majority, its leader was not recalled to power until August 23; and he was dismissed once more by the King on October 5, immediately after he had obtained a vote of confidence from the Chamber at the close of a momentous debate on foreign policy. The Government of Alexander Zaimis, who succeeded Mr. Venizelos in the premiership, depended on the support of the Venizelist majority; and when this support was withdrawn and the Zaimis Government was replaced by the extra-parliamentary ministry of Stephen Skouloudis, which proceeded to dissolve the Chamber, Mr. Venizelos claimed that this second dissolution within less than a year over the same issue was unconstitutional and refused to participate in the general election of December 19, 1916. This fateful decision drove the largest political party in the state into extra-parliamentary opposition and thus exacerbated the constitutional conflict into a veritable revolutionary situation. Yet it was, under the circumstances, the only possible answer to a policy which tended to establish the supremacy of the Crown over Parliament and virtually abolished constitutional government. It can be argued, in defense of this perversion of the constitution, that it was politically imperative

[4] *Ibid.*, pp. 113–28.

because it was designed to prevent the premature and unconditional participation of Greece in the World War. King Constantine's apologists, however, have also claimed that it was unassailable on constitutional grounds since the right of the King to "appoint and dismiss his ministers" and to dissolve Parliament is unlimited.[5] This claim, as Mr. Venizelos has conclusively shown, can be refuted by a correlated reading of all the articles of the constitution pertaining to the powers of the Crown, and is, moreover, contrary to the custom established by half a century of constitutional government.[6] But while George I had been content during his long reign to substitute influence for power in domestic politics, he had enjoyed undisputed primacy in the field of international relations. Hence, his successor had likewise the custom of the constitution on his side when he insisted on a decisive voice in the most vital issues of foreign policy that had ever confronted the Greek nation. At the same time, he must have been aware that his constitutional irresponsibility would not immunize him against the political consequences of his course. He repeatedly defied Parliament because he was accountable to the nation, to God, and to history. The judgment of all three was hastened by the accelerated tempo of a world crisis; and it was determined by forces and circumstances quite beyond the control of the King, the Prime Minister, and the people of Greece.

III

While neutral Greece had a large stake in a war which was bound to effect profound readjustments in the Balkans and in the Mediterranean countries, her strategic position made her attitude a matter of vital concern to the belligerent powers. And because the three major states of the one belligerent group were also the guarantors of her international and constitutional status, while she was bound by close dynastic ties to Germany, the leader of the other group, the constitutional conflict over foreign policy between her King and his Prime Minister was

---

[5] Articles XXXI and XXXVII, Constitution of 1864; G. Finlay, *History of Greece*, VII, 348, 349.

[6] Articles XXIX–XLIV, Constitution of 1864; *ibid.*, pp. 348–50.

merged in a world-wide struggle for power. What distinguished Greece from all other participants in this struggle was the fact that she was driven into it long before she formally abandoned her neutrality. She was rent into two increasingly irreconcilable factions which were hypnotized into the belief that the interests of the nation were identical with those of the group and the "cause" they happened to champion. Subjected to propaganda and to pressure from both sides, she made so many concessions to their real or alleged strategic needs, that her territory and her territorial waters, while still nominally neutral, were among the major theaters of the war. Because of her strategic importance, her relative defenselessness, and the passionate partisanship of her people she was exposed to intervention by the two belligerent alignments which were contending for world mastery. But unlike Spain in 1936–39, she suffered infinitely more at the hands of the coalition dominated by the two Western powers which claimed to be fighting for democracy and national self-determination and which were also the chief guarantors of her independent statehood.

It should be pointed out, however, that not all the members of the Franco-British coalition were equally active participants in the coercion of Greece. Czarist Russia, the third of the guarantor powers, followed the French and British lead with obvious reluctance both because of dynastic solidarity with King Constantine and because she feared that Greek participation in the war might be rewarded by the sacrifice of vital Russian interests. Moreover, after the March Revolution, the Kerensky regime refused to associate Russia with the coercive measures of the Western Allies, condemned intervention as an "inadmissible" interference in the domestic affairs of the Greek people, and urged radical revision of the policy of the Entente powers toward Greece.[7] Italy, the fourth major member of the Entente coalition, had no legal grounds for intervention because she was not one of the guarantor powers. Nevertheless, she proclaimed

---

[7] Driault, *Histoire diplomatique de la Grèce de 1821 à nos jours*, V, 290–91, 299. See also documents in the *Russian White Book,* and Phocas Cosmetatos, *The Tragedy of Greece*, trans. by E. W. and A. Dickes, pp. 279, 281, 290.

her "moral solidarity" with whatever diplomatic action her Allies considered necessary against Greece and "actively participated in the blockade of the Greek ports and all the measures agreed upon by the General Staffs of the Allies with a view to ensuring the safety of their troops on the Macedonian front."[8] In point of fact, though she contributed to these coercive measures, Italy hoped that they would not compel Greece to abandon her neutrality. While Great Britain and France blew hot and cold about the usefulness of Greece as an ally, Italian diplomacy was unswervingly opposed to Mr. Venizelos's effort (so reminiscent of Cavour's offer of Piedmontese support to the Western Allies in the Crimean War) to range his country on the side of the powers which were fighting against its traditional enemies and which he was unshakably convinced would dictate the peace. For the hard-headed directors of Italian policy realized that whereas Greece could be treated with scant consideration at the Peace Conference if she remained obstinately neutral, as a member of the victorious coalition she not only would advance an irresistible claim to the Dodecanese but also would secure restoration of the Greek territory occupied during the war by Italian troops for ostensibly strategic purposes. Hence, Italy was able in all sincerity to proclaim her sympathy for King Constantine and for his policy of neutrality; and though she pocketed (and, unlike Great Britain and France, could be suspected of hoping to keep) the not inconsiderable territorial benefits of intervention, she escaped the odium incurred by her Allies with the royalist and pro-neutrality section of the Greek people.

Thus it was Great Britain and France that took the initiative in enforcing a policy of cumulative intervention and coercion which violated all the aspects of independent statehood that might have been conceivably included in the "guarantee" they had given to Greece. They occupied parts of Greek Macedonia and Epirus and several of the Aegean and Ionian Islands. They made repeated landings in other parts of Greece, including the

[8] Driault, *op. cit.*, pp. 257–77, and Miller, *A History of the Greek People, 1821–1921*, p. 154.

capital. They resorted to what amounted to a hunger blockade in order to compel the Greek Government to accept such demands as the disarmament of the light units of the Greek navy, the withdrawal of the large part of the Greek army to the Peloponnesus, and the surrender of its equipment, the control of all means of transport and communication to the Allies, and free passage for their troops through Greek territory. They established a Franco-British superpolice in Athens and an elaborate Intelligence Service throughout the country. They proclaimed through their generals and admirals martial law in Greek cities, and secured the deportation of Greek citizens and the expulsion of the diplomatic representatives of the Central Powers with which Greece was officially at peace. They dictated to successive Greek Governments on such fundamental matters as the holding of parliamentary elections and the choice of ministers, military commanders, and administrative officials. And they ended by deciding the fate of the Crown and imposing their decision on a hopelessly divided nation.[9] These increasingly punitive measures, which amounted to "undeclared" war, impaired to the point of extinction the sovereignty, the territorial integrity, and the neutrality of Greece. That they should have been resorted to by the powers which were admittedly the most liberal and democratic of the belligerents of 1914–18 is a sufficiently disturbing phenomenon. Still more disturbing is the extent to which the methods they pursued foreshadowed the technique of international lawlessness which was evolved two decades later by the unsatisfied, anti-democratic, and warrior states, and against which the satisfied and essentially pacific democracies seem unable to devise effective means of common defense.

While this interventionist and coercive policy was made possible by Franco-British control of the Mediterranean and the extreme vulnerability of Greece to superior sea power, it would be a mistake to regard it as entirely founded on brute force.

[9] Driault, *op. cit.*, pp. 289, 295–305. For the collective note addressed to the Greek Government by the Allies and the Government's reply, see Great Britain, Foreign Office, *British and Foreign State Papers*, CX, 890 and 892. Cf. *Venizelos*, pp. 301–2; Headlam-Morley, *Studies in Diplomatic History*, p. 140, and Phocas Cosmetatos, *op. cit.*, pp. 187–89, 253–89.

It derived whatever moral sanction it had from the consent of a large section of the Greek people. It was in fact approved, encouraged and even instigated by those Greeks who believed with Mr. Venizelos that whichever side won the war Greece was bound to lose if she persisted in a policy of neutrality; that she should therefore align herself with the Franco-British coalition and thereby also support her Balkan ally Serbia, even though her treaty obligations did not commit her to such support in case of extra-Balkan hostilities;[10] that whereas her territorial integrity might be seriously menaced if at the end of the war she was not a member of the victorious coalition, her timely alignment with it would enable her to fulfill the Irredentist aspirations of Hellenism; that France and Britain were animated by their traditional friendship for the Greek people, and that their coercive measures were dictated by the exigencies of a desperate struggle and directed against a wrongheaded and badly advised king; and that the impairment of sovereignty and liberty, which these measures entailed, respectively, for the Greek state and for its citizens, should be gladly consented to for the sake of the great benefits to be derived by the entire nation, both within and beyond the borders of Greece, from partnership with the victorious powers. It was this line of reasoning that drove Mr. Venizelos, who had begun as the defender of the constitution against the King, to violate it flagrantly by such acts as the invitation to the Allies to land troops in Salonica and the successful incitement of one-half the country to secession.[11] Foreign powers engaged in a life-and-death struggle cannot have felt much compunction about treating Greece as a vassal state, when her foremost statesman, supported by a large part of her people, was their eager accomplice and did not hesitate to sacrifice her sovereignty in order to save her territorial integrity and to promote her expansion.

[10] *The Cambridge History of British Foreign Policy*, ed. by Ward and Gooch, III, 511, and Gibbons, *op. cit.*, p. 214.
[11] Driault, *op. cit.*, pp. 260 ff., and *The Cambridge History of British Foreign Policy*, III, 511. Cf. Gibbons, *op. cit.*, pp. 278–300; Cosmetatos, *op. cit.*, pp. 219–25; Miller, *op. cit.*, pp. 157–58.

Chapter Eight

POST-WAR DEVELOPMENTS[1]

I

THE RESTORATION of George II to the throne of Greece, in November, 1935, closed a crowded chapter of Greek history, which began more than twenty years earlier, when his father, King Constantine, opposed the plans of Premier Venizelos to intervene in the World War on the side of the Allied powers. The first phase of the ensuing struggle included the establishment of an insurgent Venizelist government in Salonica, the expulsion of the King by the Allies, his replacement by his second son, Alexander, and the triumph of the interventionist policy of Venizelos. The second phase terminated with the general election of November, 1920, when, despite the victorious outcome of the war and the rich rewards of the Treaty of Sèvres, Venizelos was decisively defeated and, by an overwhelming plebiscitary vote, King Constantine was restored to the throne vacated by Alexander's sudden death. A third and decisive landmark was reached in September, 1922, when the prosecution of the campaign in Anatolia even after the withdrawal of Allied support led to the defeat of the Greek army, the establishment of the Plastiras military dictatorship, the King's definitive abdication and banishment, and the influx of more than a million refugees. The pronounced Venizelist and

[1] This reproduces, with minor changes, a report entitled "Post-War Politics in Greece" prepared by the author for the Foreign Policy Association, Inc., and published by it on Sept. 1, 1936, as No. 12, Vol. XII "Foreign Policy Reports." Thanks are due to the Association for its permission to reproduce the paper. The author intended to reword the material in this report so that it might serve as an Epilogue to the present study. He died before this could be done. The editors have left the text unmodified, except for slight editorial changes and the omission of the last three pages, which are not related to the subject of this book. References in succeeding footnotes are not included in the Bibliography.—The editors.

anti-monarchist sympathies of these refugees enabled the Republicans to cut short the reign of George II, to proclaim the Republic by the vote of a partisan National Assembly, and to ratify this action by the plebiscite of April 13, 1924.

Thus the Greek monarchy, like the Austro-Hungarian, the Prusso-German, the Russian, and the Ottoman monarchies, may be regarded as a victim of the war and its revolutionary aftermath. But, while in other countries where the monarchical regime succumbed to defeat and revolution the reaction against democracy and republicanism has taken the form of essentially anti-monarchical dictatorships, the revolutionary cycle in Greece led eventually in 1935 to the restoration of the monarchy with the constitutional impress which it bore before the Constantine-Venizelos conflict. It is proposed to analyze the events which led to the restoration and to explain the deviation of Greece from the apparently normal post-war pattern of European politics, and also to indicate the changes which have taken place in the traditional foreign policy of Greece under the Republic.

II

The Greek Republic was not grounded in widespread popular opposition to the monarchy as an institution. It emerged from a military disaster which marked the end of a century of Irredentist expansionism, and for which King Constantine was held responsible by a large part of the defeated army and the Greek people. Because of its origins, the Republic became identified with the statesman who since 1915 had been the King's foremost antagonist. Yet Venizelos had never been a doctrinaire Republican. His opposition to Prince George, who was High Commissioner of Crete from 1898 to 1906, did not make him an enemy of the dynasty. When he left Crete in 1910 to assume the Greek premiership, he made it unmistakably clear that he regarded constitutional monarchy as the ideal form of government for Greece; and he adhered to this conviction despite his bitter personal hostility to King Constantine. In 1923, while he represented defeated Greece at the Lausanne Conference, he remonstrated with the revolutionary Government for banishing King Constantine's successor. But when he recognized, during his brief premiership early in 1924, that the Republic might conceivably be a way out of the revolutionary situation created by the Asia Minor disaster, he urged that the issue be decided by a plebiscite rather than by a decree of a so-called National Assembly in the election of which the royalists had not participated. Although his advice was rejected and the plebiscite of April 13, 1924 was merely confirmatory, the Republican majority of 758,762 was overwhelmingly composed of his followers, just as the 323,424 votes cast for the monarchy belonged to the normally anti-Venizelist section of the country. Precisely because to the Republican rank and file—possibly more than one-half the Greek people—the Republic was synonymous with Venizelos, it did not command the allegiance of the other half, whose loyalty to King Constantine's memory was as intense as their hostility to the Cretan statesman.

Hence the retirement of Venizelos from active politics was desired both by his enemies and by the more independent of his former lieutenants, who were anxious to depersonalize the Republican regime in order to make it acceptable to the royalist section of the Greek people. The coalition government of party leaders under the premiership of M. Zaïmis, which inaugurated the return to parliamentarism after the shortlived dictatorship of General Pangalos in September, 1926, made considerable progress in that direction and brought the revolutionary period to a close by completing the drafting of the Republican Constitution in June, 1927. But like most coalitions, it proved an increasingly cumbersome instrument of government and was already in process of disintegration when Venizelos, after an absence of four years, suddenly returned to active politics and resumed the leadership of the Liberal Party. Appointed to the premiership by President Koundouriotis on July 3, 1928, he dissolved the Chamber of Deputies, abolished proportional representation by presidential decree and held a general election on August 19, which secured for him a majority over all other parties and enabled him to govern during four turbulent years whose balance sheet showed considerable constructive achievement.

The re-emergence of Venizelos not only exasperated the royalists and slackened the pace of adherence to the Republic, but also alienated MM. Kaphandaris and Papanastassiou, his former lieutenants, and marked the beginning of the rift with General George Kondylis which was to grow into irreconcilable enmity. These Republican leaders naturally resented their relegation to a secondary role and the highhanded change of the electoral law which reduced their groups in the Chamber to virtual impotence. The Republican front was thus broken; and during the four years of the premiership of Venizelos the royalists, who combated him not only as head of the government but also as the embodiment of the Republican regime, received aid and comfort from his former followers, who were much more Republican than he was. The Republic was thus reduced once more to exclusive dependence on the Liberal Party and its leader, and the situation became the more precarious because the deflationary and restrictive measures necessitated by the repercussions of Great Britain's abandonment of the gold standard undermined the Premier's popularity and made renewal of his mandate for a second four-year term extremely problematical.[2]

Fears that the defeat of Venizelos might endanger the Republic were dispelled when Tsaldaris, the leader of the traditionally royalist Populist Party, promised unequivocally to recognize the regime and to conduct his government within its framework. In the general election of September 25, 1932, which followed this declaration, the Liberal Party secured 102 seats, in contrast to 96 seats for the Populist Party (Tsaldaris); 15 for the Progressive (Kaphandaris); 11 for the Farmer-Labor Party (Papanastassiou); 6 for the Agrarian (Mylonas) and 6

[2] For a discussion of the measures taken by Greece to meet the situation created by England's abandonment of the gold standard cf. Arnold J. Toynbee, *Survey of International Affairs, 1931*, p. 122.

for the National Radical Party (Kondylis). Protracted negotiations having failed to produce a coalition government, Tsaldaris, who had in the meantime reiterated his pledge of loyalty to the Republic, formed on November 5, 1932, what was in effect a minority government, which Venizelos agreed to tolerate. The truce lasted only until January 13, 1933, when Venizelos attacked the Government's financial policy and compelled Tsaldaris to resign and throw off his irksome tutelage. Venizelos resumed the premiership, dissolved the Chamber on the ground that its composition precluded the formation of a strong government, and decreed what was to prove a fateful general election.

The outcome of this election, held on March 5, 1933, showed that Venizelos had misread the trend of public sentiment as disastrously as he had in November, 1920. His party's strength was reduced from 102 to 96 members, while the Populist Party secured 135 seats, a clear majority in a total membership of 248. On the assumption that all the votes cast for the Populist Party and for General John Metaxas's Free Opinion Party were royalist, the royalist vote aggregated 40.33 percent of a total poll of 1,141,331.[3] But in view of Tsaldaris's reiterated pledges of loyalty to the Republic, the increment of the royalist poll was conceivably derived from normally Republican votes and might indicate dissatisfaction with four years of Venizelist rule and several months of tortuous maneuvering rather than a sudden recrudescence of royalist sentiment.

This view, which prevailed among Republican politicians, was not shared by the faction of Republican soldiers led by General Nicholas Plastiras. His attempt at a military coup on March 5–6 was a dismal failure and was liquidated by a military directorate under General Othoneos, which made way four days later for a parliamentary government headed by Tsaldaris. But this abortive resort to illegality in behalf of the Republic rad-

[3] This compared with 35.39 percent of 1,171,637 in November, 1932; 33.03 percent of 1,017,281 in August, 1928; and 39.87 percent of 921,226 in September, 1926.

ically altered the complexion of Greek politics. Although aimed at Tsaldaris and designed to deprive him of the fruits of his electoral victory, the coup occurred while Venizelos was still in power, was led by his most faithful henchman, and hence exposed him to the charge of weakness for failing to forestall it or, worse, the suspicion of connivance. Besides discrediting the foremost Republican leader, the re-emergence of General Plastiras, the head of the revolutionary government of September, 1922, revived passions which had been largely appeased by the orderly functioning of the Republican regime, and played into the hands of the irreconcilable royalists. It also drove Plastiras's old enemy, General Kondylis, the leader of the rival faction of Republican soldiers, definitely into the anti-Venizelist camp. By making Kondylis Minister of War and Admiral Hadjikyriacos, another anti-Venizelist Republican, Minister of the Navy, Tsaldaris offered tangible proof of his claim that his government, although anti-Venizelist, had no designs against the Republic.

The consequences of Plastiras's abortive coup dogged Tsaldaris's premiership and largely determined the course of Greek politics during the next two years. A motion to impeach Venizelos on the ground of complicity with the coup was made by General Metaxas in the Chamber of Deputies. While the storm it provoked was at its height, an attempt was made on the life of Venizelos, on June 6, 1933, which resulted in the death of his bodyguard and the wounding of his wife. This crime brought about the reconciliation of Venizelos with his former lieutenants, the reconstruction of a united Republican front, and the revival of the irrepressible conflict over the regime. On July 2 the reunited Republicans defeated the government's attempt to increase its majority by capturing the twenty Republican seats of Salonica through a by-election of questionable legality. At the same time, the opposition's charges that influential members of the Populist Party were implicated in the attempt on Venizelos's life and its insistence on a fearless inquiry and a speedy trial, engendered intense bitterness and made the adjustments and compromises necessitated by the Government's lack of a majority in the Senate increasingly difficult.

This was particularly the case with two major government measures: a new electoral bill establishing the majority system of election by single-member constituencies, and designed, according to the opposition, to alter the balance of power by gerrymandering normally Republican constituencies; and a bill providing for radical revision of the *cadres* of the army, navy and air force. The Republican opposition claimed that both of these measures were fraught with menace for the regime. Their rejection by the Senate, which had retained its Venizelist majority owing to its peculiar composition,[4] provoked a violent outcry among the ministerialists against the alleged obstruction of democratic government by that body. The ministerial campaign for abolition of the Senate produced, in turn, opposition charges that this intended violation of the Constitution was designed to remove the most formidable obstacle to the overthrow of the Republic. When the bills were finally passed by the Chamber over the Senate's veto, President Zaïmis refused to heed Republican exhortations to exercise a veto power he did not possess; and this refusal aroused in certain Republican quarters opposition to his reëlection and revived agitation in favor of Venizelos's candidacy. The latter's intimation that he might accept the presidency if it were endowed with powers similar to those of its American counterpart[5] not only strengthened the government's determination to oppose his candidacy but also aroused misgivings among those Republicans who feared that the assumption of the highest office in the country by the strongest personality in Greek politics would convert the parliamentary into a presidential Republic. The government's promise to replace the pending electoral bill with one more

---

[4] Ninety-two members of the Senate were elected for nine years and renewed by one-third every three years; 18 were elected by professional groups for three years; and ten were elected by both chambers in joint session for the duration of the term of the Chamber of Deputies.

[5] Letter to *Eleftheron Vima* (Athens), Sept. 22, 1934, quoted in *The Times* (London), Sept. 23, 1934.

acceptable to the opposition induced seventeen Senators to transfer their votes to President Zaïmis, who was accordingly reelected on October 19, 1934, for a five-year term in a joint session of the Chamber of Deputies and the Senate, by 197 votes out of the total 365, with 112 blank ballots, presumably cast by the Republicans.[6]

The relaxation of political tension which followed Zaïmis's reëlection and the return of the Republican opposition to the Chamber was terminated by the opening of the long-deferred trial of the persons who were accused of the attempt on Venizelos's life. Before the trial could be completed public attention was diverted from it by the sudden outbreak, on March 1, 1935, of a large-scale mutiny of the armed forces, which produced violent political repercussions. The revolt was organized by Republican officers who had been placed on the retired list since the Plastiras coup or were determined to avert such a fate, which they felt to be imminent. Convinced that their shelving was part of the Government's plan to de-Republicanize the armed forces and thus prepare the way for the restoration of the monarchy, these officers identified their professional interests with the Republican cause; and far from regarding themselves as rebels, they felt that they were the true defenders of the Republic against the designs of a crypto-royalist administration.

The insurgents' appeal to Venizelos to assume the political leadership of the movement confronted him with a fateful choice. By his own admission, he had known of the preparations of the naval officers to seize the fleet, and he had already withdrawn his objections to such action in December, 1934, but had advised his followers to wait "until they [the Government] attempt to restore the monarchy."[7] It must have been this commitment, without which the revolt might conceivably not have broken out, rather than, as he claimed, his indignation at the premature suspension of the Constitution by the Government,

[6] *The Times* (London), Oct. 15, 20, 1934.
[7] Interview with the *Manchester Guardian Weekly*, June 21, 28, 1935.

which compelled him to throw in his lot with the insurgents. The situation created by this decision gave the revolt a striking resemblance to the "National Defense" movement organized by Venizelos in 1916 to compel King Constantine to abandon his policy of neutrality. But this resemblance was superficial. Whereas in 1916 Venizelos's interventionist stand on the war had evoked passionate mass support and he was able to operate from Salonica under the protection, although with only the reluctant support, of the Allies, he was now faced by a strong Government and a hostile nation. For even those who had followed him blindly for years were bewildered and antagonized by his latest move and substantially agreed with the Government's description of the revolt as "an attempt made against the legal State by a minority of dissatisfied officers."[8] But the characterization of the insurgents as "friends of the opposition" was not quite accurate, for not only did all the Republican leaders of any prominence deplore and denounce the revolt, but even those Republicans who were convinced that the Government was heading toward the restoration of the monarchy did not believe that the rebellion of the armed forces was the best method of averting that danger.[9] Thus, Venizelos, who was a Cretan revolutionary in his twenties, exposed himself to the charge of "ending his career as he began,"[10] but with much more dubious justification. Because he had failed to clarify the issue and prepare public opinion for his action, he found himself at the head of a military and naval mutiny which, completely lacking popular support, speedily collapsed before the superior forces of the Government.

The revolt of March, 1935, was a repetition on a much larger scale of the Plastiras coup of March, 1933. That first attempt to nullify by force the anti-Venizelist electoral victory precipitated an anti-Republican campaign and provoked a series of measures which within two years drove their more immediate

[8] Quoted by Venizelos in the *Manchester Guardian Weekly,* June 21, 1935.
[9] *Kathimerini* and *Proia* (Athens), March 2, 3, 1935. *Atlantis* (New York), March 5, 7, 30, 1935.
[10] *The Times* (London), editorial, March 9, 1935.

victims to a second attempt to "save" the Republic. The failure of this second resort to illegality accelerated the process it was intended to check and created a revolutionary situation which culminated, within the short space of eight months, in the very event the insurgents were determined to avert—the restoration of the monarchy.

III

The immediate political problem of the anti-Venizelist parties, which were now left in complete possession of the field, was how best to capitalize the anti-Venizelist sentiment produced by the collapse of the revolt. General Metaxas, who had joined the Government as Minister-without-Portfolio at the outbreak of the revolt, urged that, since it was led by Venizelos and was organized in defense of the Republic, the logical consequence of its failure should be the political extirpation of Venizelism and the restoration of the monarchy. Premier Tsaldaris and General Kondylis, whose prestige had been immensely strengthened by the suppression of the revolt, favored, at first, a policy of greater leniency toward the insurgents and caution on the issue of the regime. Owing to this divergence of views, General Metaxas resigned from the Government, placed himself at the head of the restorationists and, by holding over Tsaldaris's head the threat of disruption of the Populist Party, goaded him into a policy which linked the liquidation of the revolt with the fate of the Republic.

This policy was formulated in three constituent acts submitted to the Chamber when it reassembled on March 29, with only 40 Republicans present, and passed on April 1. The first of these acts, "taking cognizance of the expressed will of the Greek people to consolidate the Republican regime," decreed the dissolution of the Chamber of Deputies and the abolition of the Senate, the appointment of a committee to draft a new Republican constitution, and the ratification of this document by the new Chamber. The second constituent act suspended the permanency of judges and public prosecutors in order to enable the Government to purge the judiciary; and the third, with the same end in view, suspended the permanency of civil servants.[11] Thus, while the Government moved, on the one hand, to revise the constitution with the professed aim of strengthening the Republic, through the operation of the second and third constituent acts it deprived the regime of its essential foundations. For the retirement of 1,200 officers and thousands of civil servants—from diplomats, university professors, and members of the Council of State to elementary school teachers and justices of the peace[12]—created in effect an "anti-Venizelist State" and placed the Republic in the keeping of its enemies.[13]

The influence of the royalist die-hards was exerted most effectively during the campaign for the election of a new National Assembly. The first constituent act of April 1, although it violated the constitution by abolishing the Senate, expressly stated that the contemplated constitutional revision was designed to strengthen the Republican regime. Yet this unequivocal declaration did not close the issue, for the Government could not afford to hand over to General Metaxas the exclusive championship of the monarchist cause. Hence, in the course of the campaign not only Tsaldaris but also Kondylis, whose presence in the Government both before and after March, 1935, had been regarded as guaranteeing the safety of the Republic, repeatedly promised that in case a majority of the National Assembly favored a change of regime, provision for a plebiscite would be made by the Government.[14, 15]

Although the issue of the regime was thus clearly raised both by the Government and by General Metaxas, the Republican leaders urged their followers to abstain from the general elec-

[11] *Kathimerini, Proia, The Times* (London), April 2, 1935.
[12] *The Times* (London), Nov. 4, 1935.
[13] The pressure of the irreconcilables was strikingly reflected in the treatment of the insurgents. The leaders of the revolt, including Venizelos and Plastiras, were sentenced to death *in absentia;* and three essentially retaliatory death sentences were carried out. On the other hand, all the Republican leaders who had not fled were acquitted except M. Gonatas, president of the Senate, who received a prison sentence of five years.
[14, 15] Campaign speeches of April 26 and May 19, 1935, *The Times* (London), April 27, May 31, 1935.

tion of June 9, claiming that the continuance of martial law, press censorship, and other repressive measures made free elections impossible.[16] Hence the election narrowed down to a contest between the Tsaldaris-Kondylis coalition, which obtained a popular vote of 671,925 out of a total of 1,074,479 and 287 seats in the Chamber out of a total of 300, and General Metaxas's "Royalist Union," which secured 147,245 votes, with only 7 seats in the Chamber.[17]

The outcome of the election was hailed by all the Republican leaders as a "resounding repudiation" and "the definitive burial of the monarchy." General Metaxas, on the other hand, claimed that his party's poor showing was due to the fact that the bulk of royalist voters had been coerced into voting for Government candidates and that the huge Government majority was therefore predominantly royalist. He accordingly called upon Tsaldaris to dispense with the formality of a plebiscite and proceed to restore the monarchy by a "sovereign act" of the National Assembly, "in accordance with a mandate it had just received from the Greek people."[18]

Tsaldaris was now faced with a difficult choice. Had he been resolutely determined to defend the Republic, he could have found in his triumph over Metaxas ample warrant for interpreting the election as a Republican victory and declaring the issue of the regime closed. This, however, would have driven the militantly royalist elements of his own party to join either Metaxas or Kondylis, who had already made a determined bid for royalist support by announcing in unequivocal terms his conversion to the monarchy.[19] On the other hand, should Tsaldaris adopt General Metaxas's suggestion, rule out the plebiscite as redundant, and restore the monarchy by decree of the Na-

[16] A. Mihalacopoulos in *Eleftheron Vima,* June 5, 1935.
[17] The rest of the poll was distributed among the Communists (86,674) and all the anti-Venizelist Republicans, led by Philip Dragoumis (70,719), with 47,714 blank ballots. Official returns, *Eleftheron Vima,* June 11, 1935.
[18] Statements by Republican leaders and by General Metaxas, *Eleftheron Vima,* June 11, 1935.
[19] Interview with the Avala News Agency, *Eleftheron Vima,* June 21, 1935.

tional Assembly, he would be violating the palpable verdict of the election. The Premier attempted to escape from this dilemma by proposing a plebiscite, a course which both he and General Kondylis had considered during the campaign only in the event of a widespread popular demand for restoration.[20] On July 9 he submitted to the National Assembly a resolution which provided for a plebiscite, to be held before November 15, to decide between the maintenance of the parliamentary Republic and the restoration of "constitutional monarchy under a system of parliamentary government"; and decreed, in the event of a verdict favorable to the monarchy, the return of the Glücksburg dynasty "in the recognized male line of succession."[21]

The resolution was passed by a comfortable majority after an unexpectedly spirited debate which, in effect, inaugurated an anti-Venizelist campaign in defense of the Republic. The most spectacular aspect of this campaign was the defection from the monarchist ranks of prominent men belonging to the younger generation of anti-Venizelists, whose family antecedents should have made them bitterly hostile to the Republican regime.[22] These conversions were symptomatic of a widespread popular movement on behalf of the Republic. In the course of the summer a mounting volume of protest against the Government's policy and expressions of devotion to the regime came from many quarters—professional and business groups, organized labor, even the traditionally royalist peasantry, and above all "from the intellectual and discerning classes of society."[23] Fear that this mobilization of Republican sentiment might jeop-

[20] Cf. p. 150.
[21] *Eleftheron Vima,* July 9, 1935.
[22] These eleventh-hour converts included Professor P. Kanellopoulos of the University of Athens, a nephew of D. Gounaris, the founder of the Populist Party and a victim of "revolutionary justice" in November, 1922; M. A. Stratos, whose father, Nicholas Stratos, shared the same fate, and who resigned his seat in the Chamber because he felt that he had been elected under the erroneous impression that he was a monarchist; and M. P. Dragoumis, whose brother, Ion Dragoumis, the foremost intellectual leader of anti-Venizelism, was a victim of police brutality during the World War.
[23] *Hestia* (Athens), quoted in *The Times* (London), Sept. 6, 1935.

ardize the outcome of the plebiscite impelled the militant restorationists among Tsaldaris's followers to turn to General Kondylis as the ideal leader for a "dynamic" settlement of the issue. This alliance between the energetic ex-Republican and the ultra-royalist politicians and soldiers was cemented while the Premier was taking his annual "cure" in Germany. Utilizing to the full his position as Minister of War as well as Acting Premier, General Kondylis made the necessary military preparations for a preliminary coup designed to force the Premier to abandon his neutrality. When General Panayotakos, commander of the Athens garrison, attempted to checkmate these plans on the very day of Tsaldaris's return, General Kondylis accused him of insurbordination and tendered his resignation. The Premier missed his last opportunity to rid himself of his dangerous associate. In order to induce the War Minister to withdraw his resignation, he removed General Panayotakos from the command of the Athens garrison, thus yielding control of that crucial position to the restorationists, and on September 11 he followed, after a three-month delay, in General Kondylis's footsteps by announcing his adherence to the monarchy. This surrender cost him the support of the Republicans without winning over the royalist die-hards, who still differed with him on the all-important question of procedure. For although finally compelled to repudiate the Republic, Tsaldaris clung steadfastly to the terms of the decree of July 9 which provided for the settlement of the question by a plebiscite. His position with respect to the restoration of the monarchy was, in other words, the same as that of Venizelos early in 1924 with regard to its abolition. The ultra-royalists, on the other hand, like General Kondylis and the other Republican extremists in 1924, insisted on abolition of the Republic by decree of the National Assembly, to be followed by a confirmatory plebiscite.

It was on this issue that Tsaldaris fought his last battle and made his final surrender. Successive dismissals and transfers, which had been accelerated since the revolt of March, 1935, had removed not only Republican but even moderate royalist officers from the fighting services, and the way had thus been prepared for a successful royalist coup. On October 10 a deputation of officers consisting of General Papagos, commander of the Athens garrison, Rear Admiral Economou, and Colonel Repas, commander of the air corps, confronted Tsaldaris with the alternative of capitulation to their demand for immediate restoration or resignation. The Premier resigned under protest. General Kondylis immediately assumed the Premiership, convoked the National Assembly, and submitted a series of resolutions which decreed abolition of the regime of "uncrowned democracy" (that is, the Republic), holding of a plebiscite on November 3, the appointment of the Premier as Regent, and restoration of the constitution of 1911 pending the constitutional revision necessitated by these changes.[24]

Despite the relative one-sidedness of the Assembly, due to the abstention of the Republican opposition from the general election of June 9, General Kondylis was unable to muster a majority for these decrees. They were passed on the same day by what was, in effect, a rump Parliament, consisting of a minority of about 100, the majority having followed Tsaldaris, who withdrew after a speech of protest. The Premier-Regent then called on President Zaïmis to announce that his office had ceased to exist, and on October 11 M. Simopoulos, the Greek Minister in London, waited on the King to notify him of his restoration.[25]

The new Government proceeded to organize the plebiscite with a view to removing all danger of a verdict favorable to the Republic.[26] But though the government's thoroughness made an affirmative vote a foregone conclusion, the outcome of the plebiscite was startling. The total poll of 1,727,714[27] exceeded by nearly half a million the average of the elections held during the preceding eleven years. Assuming that, despite the exhortations of Republican leaders, the abstention of Republi-

[24] *Eleftheron Vima* Oct. 10, 11, 1935.
[25] *The Times* (London), Oct. 11, 1935.
[26] George Weller, New York *Times*, Nov. 2, 1935.
[27] *The Times* (London), Nov. 4, 1935.

can voters was negligible, and that the vote of the armed forces accounted for a considerable part of the increment, these figures reveal a degree of coercive and repressive control unprecedented in Greek politics. This impression is heightened by a comparison of the million and a half votes cast for the monarchy with the 33,000 cast for the Republic, and by the fact that in Crete and western Thrace, strongholds of Venizelism and Republicanism, the Republic received, respectively, only 1,214 and 1,276 votes as against 50,655 and 72,723, for the monarchy.[28]

Yet in the last analysis, there was an element of genuineness in the outcome of the plebiscite which eludes statistical tabulation. The very ominousness of the situation which made these figures possible was already producing a revulsion of feeling among Republicans which must have contributed materially to the huge size of the monarchist poll. The motive of this reversal was the hope that the restored monarchy would be both national and constitutional; that it would, in short, offer an escape from the factional dictatorship foisted on the Greek people by its restorers. In view of the notorious incompatibility of kingship with post-war dictatorship, the very completeness of General Kondylis's triumph spelled his ultimate defeat. For he now had to deal with a King, who, thanks largely to his exertions, had received an overwhelming popular endorsement, and was apparently determined to restore the unity of the nation and the rule of law which had been shattered in the process of achieving his restoration.

IV

Both before and after the plebiscite the King had given increasingly clear indications of his intentions. He went out of his way to give Venizelos the necessary assurances through Greek and foreign intermediaries[29] and to invite the coöpera-

[28] The exact figures were 1,491,992 for the monarchy against 32,454 for the Republic and 3,268 spoiled ballots. *The Times* (London), Nov. 4, 1935.

[29] One of the intermediaries seems to have been M. Laval, the French Premier, to whom the King communicated his intentions for transmission to Venizelos when he stopped in Paris on his way back to Greece. *The Times* (London), Dec. 2, 1935.

tion of the exiled and proscribed Republican leader toward a policy of reconciliation and appeasement. These advances, and the fear that continued Republican opposition might make the King the crowned head of the "anti-Venizelist State" which had restored him,[30] induced a radical change of front on the part of Venizelos. In a letter to M. Rouphos, one of his former ministers who had remained a monarchist, he prescribed for his followers an attitude of benevolent toleration toward the King, provided he granted a general amnesty and restored constitutional government and civil liberty.[31] These conditions were met by the King's promise to devote his energies to the welfare of "all his people ... to forget the past," and "to secure equality and justice for all."[32] The popular response evoked by this promise and by Venizelos's endorsement impelled the other Republican leaders to follow his lead;[33] and the restored ruler resumed his reign with the increasingly enthusiastic support of those who had most vehemently opposed his restoration.

By the same token, he disappointed those who had brought it about. The first clash between Premier Kondylis and the King occurred over the fate of those who were connected with the revolt of March, 1935. The King insisted on a general amnesty for all the civilian, and a general pardon for all the military, insurgents. The Premier and the majority of his anti-Venizelist Cabinet, however, contended that the amnesty should not be extended to Venizelos, Plastiras, and all the others who had been sentenced as leaders of the revolt.[34] This first test of strength between King and king-maker resulted in the King's favor. George II was not intimidated by demonstrations staged by the Premier's ultra-royalist supporters; he demanded and promptly received pledges of loyalty from General Papagos, commander of the Athens garrison; and above all, he had be-

[30] *The Times* (London), Dec. 5, 1935, and letter of Venizelos to the *National Herald* (New York), Dec. 12, 1935.
[31] *Eleftheron Vima*, Nov. 16, Dec. 4, 1935; *The Times* (London), Nov. 29, 1935.
[32] First Royal Proclamation, *Eleftheron Vima*, November 26, 1935.
[33] Except M. Papanastassiou, who promised to operate within the framework of the regime without, however, recognizing it formally.
[34] *Eleftheron Vima*, Nov. 28, 1935.

hind him a solid and growing body of both monarchist and Republican sentiment. General Kondylis was therefore compelled to resign, and on December 1 the King called to the premiership Constantine Demerdjis, professor of civil law at the University of Athens, who at the head of a non-party Government took the first steps toward liquidating the Kondylis dictatorship.

He began by "granting full amnesty to all the civilians and full pardon to all the officers and public functionaries who were sentenced for participation in the March revolt,"[35] and he made a promising start toward the abolition of the "anti-Venizelist State" by reinstating large numbers of civil servants, judges, and university professors who had been deposed by the Tsaldaris and Kondylis Governments.[36] The next important step in this process—the holding of free elections—was recommended to the King not only by the ex-Republicans, who were not represented in the Chamber of June 9, but also by Generals Kondylis and Metaxas, who hoped to increase their strength by a new election. The Populist Party, which dominated the Chamber, held, on the other hand, that as a constituent body the National Assembly was not subject to dissolution by royal decree and that it would dissolve itself only after it had framed a constitution for the restored monarchy.[37] The circulation of a round-robin signed by 166 deputies of the Populist Party, calling on the Speaker to convoke the Chamber over the head of the Government, brought matters to a climax. A royal decree, accompanied by an explanatory proclamation to the people, dissolved the Chamber, ordered a general election for January 26, 1936, "with the participation of all parties," and defined the task of the new parliament as "revisionist," that is, confined to the amendment of the non-essential provisions of the monarchical Constitution of 1911.[38]

[35] Premier Demerdjis's statement to the press, *Eleftheron Vima*, Dec. 1, 1935; New York *Times*, Dec. 2, 1935.
[36] *Eleftheron Vima*, Jan. 26, 1936.
[37] Tsaldaris's speech to the Populist party caucus, *Eleftheron Vima*, Dec. 16, 1935.
[38] *The Times* (London), and *Eleftheron Vima*, Dec. 18, 1935.

The general election of January 26, 1936, which was conducted by the Demerdjis Government with the utmost impartiality under a modified system of proportional representation, may be said to have terminated the revolutionary situation begun in March, 1933, which brought about the restoration of the monarchy, and the Chamber which emerged from this election was by and large a replica of the Chamber returned by the equally free election of September, 1926, which closed the revolutionary situation that attended the birth of the Republic. The most startling feature of the election was the complete recovery of the Liberal Party, which secured 126 seats, and the strong showing of the Communists, who obtained 15 seats. On the other hand, the Populist Party, the Liberal Party's traditional rival, was definitely split. Its ultra-royalist right wing, under M. John Theotokis, combined with General Kondylis to form the "Radical Union," which won 60 seats, while Tsaldaris's following was reduced to 72 seats. The balance of the 300 seats was distributed among seven small groups.[39]

Precisely because the new Chamber reflected so faithfully all sections of opinion, the task of forming a parliamentary government proved extremely arduous. Since no party had obtained a clear majority, it was generally recognized that either an ecumenical (all-party) government or a coalition of the two major parties was indicated. The latter solution was urged by the leaders of the smaller parties except M. Theotokis, General Kondylis's ally, who pointedly recalled the fate of the 1928 coalition at the hands of Venizelos, and asked for guarantees against his return to active politics.[40] The coalition plan was agreed to eagerly by Themistocles Sophoulis, Venizelos's successor as the leader of the Liberal Party, and somewhat more reluctantly by Tsaldaris, the Populist leader, who pointed out the difficulties of his position in the face of criticism from his anti-Venizelist following.[41] But after protracted negotiations, in the course of

[39] Third and final balloting. *Eleftheron Vima*, Feb. 23, 1936.
[40] Minutes of the Crown Council of Feb. 13, 1936, *Eleftheron Vima*, Feb. 15, 1936.
[41] *Ibid.*

which both leaders made considerable concessions, it was found impossible to agree on the distribution of the three defense ministries and the allocation of the Ministry of the Interior.[42] Behind this disagreement was the profound divergence of the two camps on the all-important question of the reinstatement of the Venizelist and Republican officers who had been retired since the Plastiras coup of March, 1933. M. Demerdjis, who, largely because of his lack of party affiliations, had already made an excellent beginning with his herculean task, was therefore asked to carry on; and he reconstructed his Government on March 14 by appointing General Metaxas to the War Office and the vice-presidency of the Council. After M. Demerdjis's sudden death on April 13 and the failure of a second attempt to form a Liberal-Populist coalition,[43] General Metaxas succeeded to the premiership. Although the leader of one of the small parliamentary groups, he appeared before the Chamber with a comprehensive program, the most important part of which was his promise to "restore internal peace and the rule of law"; and he pressed for immediate passage of a resolution adjourning parliament for five months and transferring its legislative functions to a permanent parliamentary commission of forty members, on which all parties were to be proportionately represented. After a long debate the Enabling Act was passed by 249 votes against 16, and M. Metaxas was authorized to govern under its terms until September 30, 1936.[44] But the situation underwent another change before the expiration of this time limit. On August 5, 1936, after three months of increasingly difficult collaboration with the parliamentary commission, the Premier invoked the threat of a general strike allegedly sponsored by Communists, declared a state of emergency pending the restoration of public order, and dissolved the Chamber without fixing a date for new elections.

[42] *Eleftheron Vima*, Feb. 22, 1936.
[43] *Ibid.*, April 24, 1936.
[44] *Ibid.*, April 28, 1936.

V

With the restoration of constitutional monarchy, the general election of January 26, 1936, and the relative appeasement achieved under the Demerdjis and Metaxas governments, the revolutionary cycle begun in 1915 appeared to be drawing to a close. By an impressive coincidence which provided a fitting conclusion, the three leaders who epitomized this period—Venizelos, its dominant figure, Tsaldaris and Kondylis, the protagonists of its last phase—died within half a year after the plebiscite of November 3.[45]

Yet, despite unmistakable symptoms of normality, the parliamentary system had not been completely restored even at the time of Premier Metaxas's coup of August 5, 1936. The Chamber elected on January 26 showed itself incapable of producing a government and was compelled to delegate its functions to a commission and to turn to a Premier who was the leader of one of its smallest groups and who owed his position more to the confidence of the Crown than to the more or less reluctant support of Parliament. The parliamentary leaders resented this anomalous position, while the Premier, in turn, was increasingly irked by the commission's vigilant control over a Government which was essentially non-parliamentary. Actually, the coup of August 5 proved a prelude to permanent dictatorship by General Metaxas.

General Metaxas does not belong to either of the types that had dominated Greek politics during the preceding twenty years. He is neither a parliamentarian like Venizelos, Gounaris, and Tsaldaris, nor a fighting general like Plastiras and Kondylis. He first came into prominence as a brilliant General Staff officer during the Balkan Wars (1912–13); and his political activities have been guided by shrewd opportunism and accurate calculation. Though one of King Constantine's closest military advisers during the World War, he disapproved of the post-war

[45] General Kondylis died on Jan. 31, Venizelos on March 18, Premier Demerdjis on April 13, and Tsaldaris on May 17, 1936.

campaign in Anatolia, dissociated himself from it, and thus escaped its disastrous consequences. After his presumably monarchist attempt against the Plastiras dictatorship in 1923 had been put down by the then Republican Kondylis, he turned to parliamentary politics. But while he made a creditable record as Minister of Communications in the Zaïmis coalition Government, he displayed neither the gifts nor the temperament of a democratic and parliamentary leader. Caught between the Populists and the Venizelists, he was unable to build a strong party; and after his defeat in the Venizelist landslide of August 19, 1928, he retired from politics and did not reëmerge until the general election of March 5, 1933. Following the suppression of the revolt of March 1, 1935, he was supplanted by Kondylis in the leadership of the extreme restorationists and seemed condemned to a secondary rôle as the leader of a small parliamentary group. But the depletion of the political ranks caused by the successive deaths of Kondylis, Venizelos, Demerdjis and Tsaldaris, combined with the King's favor, helped to elevate him to the premiership.

It is clear that Premier Metaxas's temperament, military training, and disillusioning experiences with parliamentary politics predispose him toward authoritarian government. Even before the coup of August 5 his attitude on the question of restoration of civil liberty and the policies of Colonel Skylakakis, his Minister of the Interior, left much to be desired.[46] He has included in his Cabinet, as Minister of Finance and Vice-Premier, M. Constantine Zavitsanos, a veteran but disgruntled parliamentarian who has made no secret of his preference for dictatorial rule. The closing of party headquarters, the imposition of press censorship, above all the Government's paternalism—its reiterated professions of solicitude for the masses and the offer of economic security in exchange for liberty and self-government—these and other palpable imitations

[46] Cf. memorandum of the "League for the Defense of the Rights of Man and of the Citizen," signed by eminent representatives of all classes, *Eleftheron Vima*, July 31, 1936.

of the Fascist and Nazi dictatorships should leave little doubt about the Premier's intentions. It is evident that the coup of August 5 has ushered in a new period of conflict along lines quite different from those of the preceding twenty years. This struggle between democracy and reaction, which seems imminent in Greece, does not impinge immediately upon the monarchy. Its position will be seriously affected only if the King, having acquiesced in Premier Metaxas's coup, allows himself to become permanently identified with the dictatorship it was designed to establish.

VI

If it is true that the degree of independence enjoyed by a given nation is determined in the main by its size, its material resources, its geographical location and certain traditional beliefs and attitudes which are the residue of its historical development, the independence achieved by Greece in 1830 was largely nominal.

This generalization applies particularly to the antecedents of the Republic, since, as has been pointed out, the movement for the abolition of the monarchy originated in a conflict over foreign policy and triumphed as a result of military defeat. On the other hand, the contribution of foreign policy to the restoration of the monarchy was much less decisive. Though the restoration synchronized with the Anglo-Italian conflict over Ethiopia, there was no pro-British or pro-Italian party in Greece, and the pattern of 1915–20, when the Venizelists and potential Republicans were pro-Ally and the royalists pro-German, was not repeated in 1935–36. While the assumption is warranted that the restoration was favored by Britain both for dynastic reasons and because a united Greece was needed on the anti-Italian front, it is difficult to determine to what extent British wishes in the matter influenced Greek opinion. All that can be said with any certainty is that the longing for national unity in the midst of a perilous international situation must have contributed to the restoration of the monarchy and that its consolidation was due in some measure to the feeling of security engendered by the reconciliation of the King with the nation's foremost statesman and diplomat.

An explanation of the relatively insignificant part played, for almost the first time since 1830, by international factors in a major political change may be found in the radical reorientation of Greek foreign policy under the Republic—a reorientation made possible by the fact that the Greek state has at last become more important than the Greek nation beyond its borders. Two factors have contributed most decisively to this change: the defeat of 1922 and its consequences—the end of the century-old policy of Irredentist aggrandizement and the deportation of the Greek subjects of Turkey to Greece—and the economic decline of the Greeks of the Dispersion or the gradual loss of their sense of kinship with the mother country, due to such post-war developments as the Russian Revolution, the growth of Egyptian nationalism, and the stoppage of immigration to America.[47] Thus, because Greece, after a decade of war and diplomacy (1912–22), has gathered the bulk of the Greek people within its borders, the security of the state, rather than the liberation of the "unredeemed" part of the nation, has now become the major objective of its foreign policy.

The shift of objective from aggression and aggrandizement to defense and security has enabled Greece to rid itself of its dependence on the great powers at precisely the time when the Greek people became disillusioned both with regard to the benevolence of their intentions and the efficacy of their support. For a hundred years attachment to a given great power or group of powers had been a cardinal maxim of Greek foreign policy. The "Russian," the "British," and the "French" parties which flourished during the reign of Otho were succeeded by the dynastic diplomacy of George I, who was expected to use his family connections for the furtherance of the national interests. This tradition, which culminated in the passionate pro-Ally

[47] For a discussion of this aspect of the post-war international position of Greece cf. A. J. Toynbee, "The East after Lausanne," *Foreign Affairs*, Sept. 15, 1923.

and pro-German partisanship of the World War, was practically killed by such post-war developments as the desertion of Greece by the Allies, the successful defiance of the Allies by Turkey, the fluidity of the post-war international alignments, and the growing assertiveness of the smaller states made possible by regional combinations and the League of Nations.

The new foreign policy, which has been built on these foundations of fact and national psychology, is therefore guided by the following principles: opposition to revisionism, which means respect for the territorial *status quo,* whether established by victory (Treaty of Neuilly with Bulgaria) or by defeat (Treaty of Lausanne with Turkey) ; and organization of security on a strictly regional basis, and consequent refusal to become entangled in the conflicts of the great powers or to be drawn into any commitments beyond the Balkan peninsula and the Mediterranean.

Bibliography

The titles preceded by an asterisk are translated from the Greek; the texts of the items so marked are in Greek.

Amantos, K. *Documents concerning Rhigas of Velestinos, Athens, 1930.
Andreades, A. M. *Studies in Public Economy. Athens, 1925.
Aravantinos, J. *Constitutional Law of Greece. Athens, 1897.
Argyropoulos, F. *Adamantios Koraes. Athens, 1877.
Cambridge History of British Foreign Policy, 1783–1919, The, ed. by Sir A. W. Ward and G. P. Gooch. 3 vols. Cambridge, 1922–23; New York, 1922.
Capodistrias, J., *see* Kapodistrias, I. A.
Cosmetatos, S. P. P., *see* Phocas-Cosmetatos, S. P.
Cosmin, S., pseud., *see* Phocas-Cosmetatos, S. P.
Couclelis, A. P. Les Régimes gouvernementaux de la Grèce de 1821 à nos jours. Paris, 1920.
Crawley, C. W. The Question of Greek Independence: a Study of British Policy in the Near East, 1821–1833. Cambridge, 1930.
Dascalakis, A. Rhigas Velestinlis; la révolution française et les préludes de l'independance hellénique. Paris, 1937.
——Causes and Factors of the Greek Revolution of 1821. Athens, 1927.
Dragoumes, N. *Historical Reminiscences. 2 vols. Athens, 2d ed. 1875, 3d 1925. Also in French, Souvenirs historiques, trans. by J. Blanchard. Paris, 1891.
Driault, E. Histoire diplomatique de la Grèce de 1821 à nos jours. 5 vols. Paris, 1925–26.
Du Coudray, Helene. Metternich. London, 1935; New Haven, 1936.
Eardley-Wilmot, Sir S. M. Life of Vice-Admiral Edmund Lord Lyons. London, 1898.
Finlay, G. A History of Greece from Its Conquest by the Romans to the Present Time, B. C. 146 to A. D. 1864. 7 vols. Oxford and London, 1877.
——History of the Greek Revolution. 2 vols. Edinburgh and London, 1861.

Fustel de Coulanges, N. D. La Cité antique; étude sur le culte, le droit, les institutions de la Grèce et de Rome. 28th ed. Paris, 1924. Also in translation ed. by Willard Small, The Ancient City, a Study of the Religion, Laws and Institutions of Greece and Rome. 12th ed. Boston, 1901.

Gervinus, G. G. Geschichte des neunzehnten Jahrhunderts seit den Wiener Vertragen. 8 vols. (Vols. VI and VII deal with affairs of Greece). Leipzig, 1855–66.

Gibbons, H. A. Venizelos. Boston, 1920.

Gobineau, [J. A.], Comte de. Deux études sur la Grèce moderne; Capodistrias, le royaume des Hellènes. Paris, 1905.

Great Britain, Foreign Office. British and Foreign State Papers (referred to in footnotes as B.F.S.P.), Vols. XII (1824–25), XIII (1825–26), XIV (1826–27), XV (1827–28), XVI (1828–29), XVII (1829–30), XVIII (1830–31), XIX (1831–32), XX (1832–33), XXII (1833–34), XXXII (1843–44), XXXIX (1849–50), XLI (1851–52), XLV (1854–55), LIII (1862–63), LIV (1863–64), LV (1864–65), LVIII (1867–68), CX (1916).

Guillon, E. L. M. Napoléon et la Suisse, 1803–1815. Paris, 1910.

Hansard, T. C., comp., Parliamentary Debates, Third Series, 1820–1832. London.

Headlam-Morley, Sir J. W. Studies in Diplomatic History. London, 1930.

Idromenos, A. M. *J. Capodistrias, Ruler of the Greeks. Athens, 1900.

Imperial Russian Archeological Society. Official Records. Vol. I. St. Petersburg, 1851–1916.

Jefferson, Thomas. Writings of Thomas Jefferson, ed. by H. A. Washington. 9 vols. New York, 1853–55.

Kapodistrias, I. A., Count. *Correspondence. Athens, 1841–42. Also in French translation, Correspondance du comte J. Capodistrias, président de la Grèce . . . 4 vols. Geneva, 1839.

Koraes, A., ed. Aristoteles (Politica, 1821). *Prolegomena to the Politics. Athens, 1923.

Kordatos, J. K. *Political History of Modern Greece. Athens, 1925. Vol. I.

Lascaris, S. T. Capodistrias avant la Révolution grecque, sa carrière politique juspu'en 1822; étude d'histoire diplomatique et de droit international. Lausanne, 1918. Thesis, Paris.

———La Politique exterieure de la Grèce après le Congres de Berlin (1875–81). Paris, 1924.

Letters to Thomas Jefferson. MS in files of the Department of State, United States Government, Washington, D. C.

Mamoukas, A. *Documents Relating to the Greek Renaissance. Piraeus, 1839. Vols. I and II. Athens, 1852. La Renaissance de la Grèce. 9 vols. in 3. Piraeus, 1839.

Martin, W. La Suisse et l'Europe, 1813–1814. Lausanne, 1931.

Mavrogordato, J. Modern Greece: a Chronicle and a Survey, 1800–1931. London, 1931.

Mendelssohn-Bartholdy, Karl. Geschichte Griechenlands, 1453–1870. 2 vols. Leipzig, 1874.

Metternich-Winneburg, C. L. W., Fürst von. Memoirs of Prince Metternich, 1773–1835. Ed. by Prince Richard Metternich. Trans. by Mrs. Alexander Napier. 5 vols. New York, 1881.

Mihalopoulos, P. *Rhigas of Velestinos. Athens, 1930.

Miller, W. A History of the Greek People, 1821–1921. London, 1922. History of the People's Series.

Moschovakis, N. G. *Public Law in Greece under Turkish Rule. Athens, 1882.

Muyden, B. Von. Histoire de la nation suisse. Lausanne, 1899.

Paparregopoulos, K. Histoire de la civilisation hellénique. Paris, 1878.

Philaretos, G. *Notes, 1848–1923. Athens, 1928.

Phocas-Cosmetatos, S. P. The Tragedy of Greece. Trans. by E. W. and A. Dickes. New York, 1928. Also in French, L'Entente et la Grèce pendant la grande guerre. 2 vols. Paris, 1926.

Pipinelis, T. *Political History of the Greek Revolution. Athens, 1928.

Reynold, G. de. La Démocratie et la Suisse. Bienne, 1934.

Rhigas, K. Les Oeuvres de Rhigas Velestinlis; étude bibliographique suivie d'une ré-édition critique avec traduction française de la brochure révolutionnaire, confisquée à Vienne en 1797 . . . par Ap. Dascalakis. Paris, 1937.

Saripolos, N. N. *System of Constitutional Law and General Public Law. Athens, 1903. Also in French and German translations: Systeme de droit constitutionel. Athens, 1903. Das Staatsrecht des Königreichs Griechenland. Tubingen, 1909.

Skleros, G. Contemporary Problems of Hellenism. Alexandria, 1919.

Speliades, N. *Reminiscences of the Greek Revolution. 3 vols., ed. by Philadelpheus, Athens, 1851–57.

Stern, A. Geschichte Europas seit den Verträgen von 1815 bis zum Frankfurter Frieden von 1871. 10 vols. Berlin, 1894–1924.

Strupp, C., ed. La Situation internationale de la Grèce (1821–1917). Recueil de documents choisis et édités avec une introduction historique et dogmatique. Zurich, 1918.

Temperley, H. The Foreign Policy of Canning, 1822–1827. London, 1925.
Thereianos, D. *Adamantios Koraes. 3d ed. Athens, 1890.
Thiersch, F. De l'état actuel de la Grèce. Leipzig, 1833.
Tricoupes, S. *History of the Greek Revolution. 4 vols. in 2. 3d ed. Athens, 1888.
Venizelos, Eleutherios, and others. The Vindication of Greek National Policy, 1912–17. London, 1918.

Index

Aberdeen, Lord, 109, 110; as spokesman of British and French interests, 104-7
Absolutism, uncongenial to people, 40; *vs.* constitutionalism, 102
Act of Mediation, 60, 61
Act of Submission, 39, 81
Adalbert of Bavaria, 108
Administrative system of the Revolution, 55 ff.
Admiral of the Fleet, 29, 30
Aegean Islands, under Ottoman rule, 30; upper-class attitude toward Insurrection, 42; owning class, 46; membership in National Convention, 53
Alexander, King, 5, 148
Alexander, Czar, 35; Capodistrias in service of, 59, 60-64; Swiss policy, 60; quoted, 61
Alfred, Prince, candidacy, 123 ff., 129
Amalia, Queen, 113, 114
Amiens, Treaty of, 26
Antolia, campaign in, 5, 148, 169
Appointment, power of, 99
Aristocracy's rule, 23, 24, 26; Koraes's hostility to, 14; Capodistrias's hostility, 59, 64, 67, 77
Aristotle, 12, 13
Armed forces *see* Military affairs
Athens garrison, 96, 111, 137; in control of restorationists, 161; commander's pledge to King, 164
Austria, accusations against Rhigas, 18; Capodistrias's efforts to checkmate, 62 f.
Autonomy, provincial and municipal, 28 f., 55, 56

"Battle Hymn" (Rhigas), 19, 20, 22*n*
Bavaria, Greece becomes a protectorate of, 92; affirmation of sovereignty and promise re constitution, 93; government by bureaucrats of, 96; expulsion of dynasty, 111, 113; challenges Great Britain on "guarantee," 116; lien on throne of Greece, 121, 126 f., 128; Duke of Leuchtenberg a subject of, 122; *see also* Otho
Bavaria, King of, 91, 105, 108, 109
Berthier, Marshal, 27
Bill of Rights, 52, 53
Blum, Léon, 3
Bourgeoisie, rise of, 9; represented by *Hetairia Philike*, 41
Broglie, Duke of, quoted, 94
Brotherhood, vision of universal, 20
"Byzantine Constitution," 25, 59
Byzantine Empire, nationalism reared upon grandeur of, 3; Ionian culture, 23; dream of a resuscitated, 41

Cambridge History of British Foreign Policy, quoted, 35*n*
Canning, George, 36, 38, 39, 81
Canning, Sir Stratford, 69*n*, 81
Capodistrias, Agostino, 66*n*, 88, 89
Capodistrias, John, 36, 37, 37*n*, 40, 51, 57, 80, 82, 83, 87, 90, 93; judgements passed upon, 17, 58 f.; assassination, 17, 67, 87; political noviitate in Ionian Islands, 24, 27, 59; basic constitutional problem of his administration, and his stand in resulting conflict, 58; attitude toward constitutionalism, 58, 67, 68, 71 ff., 85 ff.; political philosophy, 59, 64 ff.; views on the franchise, 59, 60, 75 78; mission to Switzerland, 60-62; share in shaping foreign policy of Russia, 62-64; conflict with Metternick, 62, 63; policies pursued as presidential dictator, 65, 71-79; faults and shortcomings, 66; stand on monarchy, 68 ff., 86

INDEX

Capodistrias, Viaro, 66n
Capoudan Pasha, 29
Castlereagh, Lord, 35, 36
Cephalonia, 59
Cetto, Baron, 116
Chamber of Deputies, King's right to dissolve, 141; bill for dissolution, 157
Chios, 32
Christianity, adherence to, a prerequisite to citizenship, 52
Civil servants, 158, 165
Civil war, outbreak in 1824, 49
Classics, series published by Koraes, 12
Clergy, upper: attitude toward the Insurrection, 42, 43
Cochrane, 51
Colocotronis, Theodore, 24; military leadership, 44, 48, 49; surrender of high command, 51
Communists, 159n, 166, 167
Concurrent powers, effect of, 49
Conference of Ambassadors, see London Conference
"Congress System," 62
Constantine, King, 156, 168; struggle between Venizelos and, 5, 140 ff., 148, 149; abdication and banishment, 6; removal from army demanded, 137; rule of, 141 ff.; defiance of Parliament and insistence upon decisive voice in foreign policy, 143; expulsion, restoration, abdication, 148; held responsible for military disaster, 149; loyalty to, 150; see also Monarchy
Constantinople, Patriarch of, 28, 103
Constitution (Rhigas), 19, 22
Constitution, American, 17
"Constitution, Byzantine," 25, 59
Constitution, French, 20, 22, 48
Constitution, Greek: experiments during Revolution, 34–57, 80; provisional, framed by first National Convention, 37, 40, 46, 47 f.; earliest, analyzed, 56; enduring ground work laid by, 57; principles embodied in all three of Revolution, 73; plans (of 1829 and 1830) for a definitive, 74, 75, 77; monarchical, formulated by fifth National Convention, 88; provisions, 88 f.; Bavarian Government's promise re, 93; attitude of the Regency, 93; rights of Assembly and King in relation to, 90; demanded by Council of State (1843), 96
— of 1827 (Troezene), 58, 68, 71, 72, 73; provisions, 51 f.
— of 1844, 97, 100; regime established by, 98 ff.; power of monarch, 101, 133, 135; influence of protecting powers, 103 ff.; their recommendations, 106; British source of inspiration, 107; perverted into instrument of autocracy, 111
— of 1864, framing of, 132–34, 136; provisions, 135 f.; orderly revision during crisis of 1909–11, 137–40
— of 1911, monarchical, 165
— of 1927, Republican, 150; appointment of committee to draft, 157
Constitution, Ionian, of 1801, 25; of 1803, 26, 27, 59
Constitutionalism, suspension of, in Europe, 3; ideology, 3, 4; sources, 9–33; writings containing basic political ideas in which grounded, 10 ff.; meaning of, to people, 40; predilection for, with reference to internal conditions of insurgent Greece, 41 ff.; futility of constitution-mongering at time of crisis, 50; Capodistrias's attitude toward, 58, 67, 68, 71 ff., 85 ff.; tradition, developed during Insurrection, 85; failure of powers to defend tradition of, 85, 87 ff.; battle against absolutism, 102; stressed in selection and installation of Danish prince, 129 ff.; crisis precipitated by World War, 140–47
Convention of May 7, 1832, 109
Convention of Sept. 14, 1843, 109
Corfu, 23n, 24
Coudray, Helene du, quoted, 63n
Council of State, 96, 134
Councils, communal and district, 78, 79
Coundouriotis brothers, 67
Coundouriotis, George, 49
Coup d'état of Sept., 1843, 96, 102, 103 f., 111

Debts, cancellation of, 21
Declaration of the Rights of Man (Rhigas), 21

Deliyoryis, E., 111
Demerdjis, Constantine, 165, 167, 168, 169
Democracies, World War conduct, later impotence, 146
Democracy, limited, of George I, 130–36; and reaction, 170
Denmark, Prince William called to Greek throne, 128; part in establishing dynastic regime, 131
Dictatorships, Capodistrian, 58–79; Metaxas, 169 f.
Dissolution of ministry, rights of Crown, 141 f.
Don Pacifico case, 109
Dragoumis, Ion, 160n
Dragoumis, M. P., 160n
Dragoumis, Philip, 159n
Dragoumis (Ion) Ministry, resignation, 138

Eastern Orthodox Church, 52; why condemned by Koraes, 11; Ionian adherence to, 23; "Romaic Nation" the Christian subjects of, 27; authority under Ottoman rule, 27–31 *passim*; made state religion, 59; rights and privileges conferred on, 80; subjected to Catholic monarch, 103; monarch must profess faith of, 108, 130, 131
Ecclesiastical hierarchy, rule by, 27–31 *passim*
Economou, Rear Admiral, 162
Education, 10, 11; Ionian Islands, 24, 25
Elections, party polls, 159, 162, 166
Electoral procedure, 26, 32, 53, 59; Provisional Electoral Law, 54; revision under Capodistrias, 59, 75–78, 79; assemblies of the Revolution, 75; electoral bill establishing majority by single-member constituencies, 154; coercive and repressive control revealed by plebiscite, 163; proportional representation, 150, 166; *see also* Franchise
Enabling acts, 72, 73, 74, 76, 167
England, government compared with that of France, 3; *see also* Great Britain
Enlightenment, the, 10, 18, 64

Equality, Koraes on, 13
Erastian Decree of 1833, 103
Europe, influence of Western, 10, 11, 27; cultural dependence on, 22; effect of ideas upon constitutions, 34, 35; importation of a king with the consent of, 37; Capodistrias's recommendations on reconstruction of, 62
Executive, constitutional provisions, 47 f., 49, 51, 52, 73

Federal Pact, The, 61
Federal state, 17
Federal system, 56
Finances, loan contracted by protecting powers, 91, 104, 110, 132; foreign dictation on policy, 109
Foreign policy, influence on domestic politics, 3 ff., 102; pressing problems preceding crisis of 1909–11, 137; changes in, under the Republic, 149 ff., 171; contribution to restoration of the monarchy, 170; principles guiding new, 172; *see also* International situation
Foreign Policy Association, Inc., 148n
France, security compared with that of England, 3; treaty "guarantee" the legal basis for intervention of, 6; Koraes's faith in, 18; Rhigas's borrowings from, 20, 22; occupation of, and influence in, Ionian Islands, 25, 27, 59; Capodistrias's attitude toward, 60, 61; opposition to him, 67; French prototype of Constitution of 1844, 101 f.; attitude toward Otho and constitutional settlement of 1844, 103 ff., 115; development of policy during Insurrection of 1862, 118 ff.; policy during World War crisis, 145–47; *see also* French Revolution; Protecting powers
Franchise, qualifications for, 25, 26, 32; first attempt at uniform, 54; Capodistrias's stand on, 59, 60, 75–78; British advise confining to Greeks, 106; *see also* Electoral procedure
French Revolution, influence of, 10, 14, 20, 22, 24, 35; repercussions felt

French Revolution (*Continued*)
throughout Greece, 22; early constitutions borrowed from literature of, 47, 52, 53
Fustel de Coulanges, N. D., quoted, 21*n*

Geographical situation, security derived from, 3
George I, King, cause for enthusiasm that greeted accession, 5; a Danish prince, 128; limited democracy of, 130-36, 141, 143, 171; election, 130, 131; share in Constitution of 1864, 134, 136; sponsors constitutional revision, 138, 139; right to dissolve Chamber of Deputies, 141; *see also* Monarchy
George II, Republic ends reign of, 6, 149; restoration to throne, 148, 163; coöperation with Venizelos, 163; contests with Kondylis, 164; policies, 164 ff.; *see also* Monarchy
George, Prince, 149
Germany, royalists pro-German, 143, 170
Gise, Baron de, 93
Glueckburg dynasty, 5; installation, 131; return of, proposed, 160
Golden Book, 23*n*, 24, 25
Gold standard, Great Britain's abandonment of, 151
Gortchakoff, Prince, 119; declaration of Russian policy, 120 ff.
Gounaris, Demetrios, 142, 160*n*, 168
Great Britain, legal basis for intervention, 6; influence in Ionian Islands, 24, 27; efforts of Mavrocordatos to commit her to Greek cause, 38; Act of Submission placing Greece under protection of, 39; opposition to Capodistrias, 67; attitude toward Othonian regime and constitutional settlement of 1844, 103 ff., 115 ff.; development of policy during Insurrection of 1862, 116 ff.; selects ruler susceptible to British influence, 125; policy during World War crisis, 145-47; abandonment of gold standard, 151; restoration of monarchy favored by, 170; *see also* Protecting powers
Greece, history shaped by ideologies of nationalism and constitutionalism, 3 ff.; influence of foreign policy, and of Irredentist movement, on domestic politics, 3, 4 ff.; conditional self-government under Ottoman rule, 4, 9, 27-33; sources of constitutionalism, 9-33; relation to decay of Ottoman institutions, 9, 32; reasons for downfall of ancient, 17; Ionian Islands' part in history of, 23-27 (*see also* Ionian Islands); bases of representative government and political and administrative organization, 33; constitutional experiments of the Revolution, 34-57; internal conditions with reference to predilection for constitutional and representative government, 41 ff.; unity of purpose achieved, 43; dictatorship of Capodistrias, 58-79; forfiture of sovereignty and surrender of self-government in exchange for independence from Ottoman rule, 80-95; robbed of internal sovereignty by Protocols of Feb. 3, 1830, 80; erected into a monarchical independent state, 91; becomes a Bavarian protectorate, 92; *coup d'état* of Sept., 1843, 96; limited monarchy of Otho, 96-110; Insurrection of 1862, 111 ff.; limited democracy of George I, 130-36; constitutional revision during crisis of 1909-11, 137-40; political and constitutional crisis precipitated by the World War, 140-47; importance to the belligerent powers of her strategic position, 143; post-war developments, 148-72; evidences of a reorientation of politics, 168; state at last more important than Irredentist aggrandizement, 171; bulk of Greek people now within own borders, 171; end of dependence on great powers, 171; principles guiding new foreign policy, 172
— continental: a propitious soil for *Philike*, 41; organized by Mavrocordatos, 46; committee representing, 48; Insurrection revived in, 50; membership in National Convention, 53

INDEX

Greek Church, *see* Eastern Orthodox Church
Greek Monarchy, The (Kolettes), 22n
Greeks of the Dispersion, 37, 41, 43, 51, 53, 171
Gregory V, Patriarch, 28

Hadjikyriacos, Admiral, 153
Hellenism, *see* Irredentist aspirations
Helvetian Republic, 60, 61
Heptanesus, 23; *see also* Ionian Islands
Hetairia Philike, 46; political eclipse, hostility of Mavrocordatos, 36; objectives and activities, 41 ff.; class affiliations and clashes, 41, 42; relation to Ypsilantis, 44, 45; leadership rejected by Capodistrias, 64
Hoidas, Roccos, 24
Holy Alliance, 17, 38
Hostages, system of government by, 28
Hydra, 48, 49, 54, 67
Hydriot shipowners, 42, 46, 49
Hobbes, Thomas, 13, 21, 87

Implied powers, assumption of, 84
Independence, War of, *see* War of Independence
Insurrection, 13, 17, 33, 50; dignitaries executed because of failure to avert, 28; world opinion on, 35; meaning of, to people and to ruling classes, 42; those who prepared, instigated, and began, 43; relationship between local officials and central government maintained, 55; salvaged by London Treaty of 1827 and victory of fleets at Navarino, 58; relation of Capodistrias to, 64, 67; intervention of the three protecting powers, 81 ff.; primary aim of, attained, 94
— *coup d'état* of Sept., 1843, 96, 102, 103 f., 107, 111
— revolt of Oct., 1862, 111 ff.; articles if decree issued, 113; development of protecting powers' policy during crisis, 116 ff.; conditions governing monarch, 129, 132; full rigor of financial obligations retained, 132
— (Young Turk) of 1908, 137
— *see also* Revolution; War of Independence
Intelligentsia, influence, 9; factors causing formation of ideas, 10; represented by *Hetairia Philike*, 41; anti-oligarchic movement preceding crisis of 1909–11, 138
International situation, relation to political development, 3, 4 ff.; constitutions of Revolution considered in relation to, 34; conditions influencing set-up of government after freedom from Ottoman rule, 35 ff., 83 ff.; leadership of Crown, 140, 143; *see also* Foreign policy
Ionian Islands, annexation, 5, 115, 125, 131; important part in history, 23–27; culture, 23; government, 23, 24–27; Capodistrias's activities, 24, 27, 59; outstanding men, 24; constitutions, 25, 26, 27, 59; relations with Greece, union in 1864, 27
Irredentist aspirations of Hellenism, 4, 10, 20, 114, 116, 117, 125, 147; as threat to Ottoman Empire, 124; Irredentas in Macedonia, 137; end of century of expansionism, 149, 171
Italy, influence in Ionian Islands, 23, 24, 26; policy during World War, 144

Jefferson, Thomas, Koraes's Jeffersonian doctrine, 15; correspondence with Koraes, 16 f.
Judiciary, permanency of, 157

Kaltchas, report prepared for Foreign Policy Association, 148n; death, 148n
Kanakares, A., 48n, 55n
Kanaris, Constantine, 113, 130; invited to form government, his proposals, 112; resignation, 113
Kanellopoulos, P., 160n
Kaphandaris, 151
Karaïskakis, campaign of, 50
"Katharevoussa," 12n
Kephallonia, 23n
King, *see* Monarchy; *also name of king*, e.g. Otho
Kodjabashis (primates), 30 ff.
Kolettes, John, 49, 98, 112; *The Greek Monarchy*, 22n
Kondylis, George, 151, 152, 153, 157, 161, 166; provision for plebiscite on change of regime, 158, 162; assumes

Kondylis, George (*Continued*)
  Premiership, 162; defeat foreshadowed, 163; contests with George II, 164; resignation, 165; death, 168, 169
Koraes, Adamantios, 10; family, career, 11; outlook and opinions, 11–18; main channels of efforts, 12; educational work of, 12–18; Jeffersonian doctrine, 15; correspondence with Jefferson, 16 f.
Koraes, Antonios, 11n
Koumoundouros, Alexander, 141
Koundouriotis, President, 150
Kyriakós, D., 98

La Harpe, 60
Landowning oligarchy, 14, 26; attitude toward *Philike*, 41, 42; toward the Insurrection, 42; national estates safeguarded against, 54; primates drawn from, 32
Language, reform of, 12, 23
Laval, M., 163n
League of Nations, 172
Legislature, constitutional provisions, 47, 49, 51, 52, 73, 133, 135; set up by first Convention, 53; membership provisions, law of 1822, 54
Leopold of Coburg, Prince, 5, 39n, 69–71, 86, 88; quoted, 70
Leuchtenberg, Duke of, 122 ff.
Lhuys, Drouyn de, 119
Liberalism *vs.* absolutism, 102
Liberal Party, 142, 150, 151, 152; dependence of Republic on, 151; recovery, 166; Liberal-Populist coalition attempted, 166 f.
Liberty, Koraes on, 13; dual conception of, 34
Literary movement, Ionian, 23
Literature of criticism and revolt, 138
Loan contracted by protecting powers, 91, 104, 110, 132
Locke, John, 13
Logothetis, J., 48n
Lombardos, Constantine, 24; quoted, 15n
London Conference, 69, 71, 110, 128; decrees form of Greek government, 80, 84; Ottoman Government to accept decisions of, 84; requests for admittance to, 86; proclamation of Aug. 30, 1832, on the monarchy, 92
London Protocols, *see* Protocols
London Treaty, *see* Treaty
Louis Philippe, King, 102, 107
Luitpold, Prince, 103, 108
Lyons, Sir Edmund, 103, 109

Macedonia, Irredentas in, 137
Mahmud II, Sultan, quoted, 28
Maina, self-government, 29; insurrection, 29, 43, 67; committee representing, 48
Mainiol, Peter, 67n
Map circulated by Rhigas, 20
Maritime islands, three, 48, 54
Mavrocordatos, Alexander, 17, 48, 55n, 97, 112; guiding principle, 36; ideas and policies, 36–39; efforts to commit Great Britain to Greek cause, 38; ideas and objectives, 45; rule of, 46 ff.
Mazzini, Giuseppe, 20
Mediation, Act of, 60, 61
Merchants, 42, 46; wealth in service of education, 10, 11
Metaxas, A., 97, 112
Metaxas, John, 152, 157, 158, 159, 165, 168, 170; dictatorship, 167, 169 f.; career, policies, 168 f.; predisposed toward authoritarian government, 169
Metternick, 35, 38, 39n, 60, 103; conflict with Capodistrias, 62, 63, 64n
Middle class, drive for power, 138
Military affairs, Peloponnesian elements, 48, 49; relations of Capodistrias toward chieftains, 67; recruiting of Bavarian corps, 92; rejection of Turkey's proposal to limit armed forces, 94, 109; Athens garrison, 96, 111, 137, 161, 164; allegiance transferred to constitutional institutions, 97; reduction of armed forces demanded by powers, 110; connivance in insurrection of 1862, 111; removal of royalty from army demanded, 137; attempt at coup of 1933, 152, 156, 167; bill re revision of the *cadres* of army, navy and air force, 154; large-scale mutiny of the armed forces, 1935, 155, 156; officers retired, 158; pardoned 165